THE COMPLETE MULTI COOKER COOKBOOK

THE COMPLETE MULTI COOKER COOKBOOK

125 deliciously easy recipes and essential techniques

Sam & Dom Milner
of KitchenGadgetsClub

WHITE LION PUBLISHING

Quarto

First published in 2026 by White Lion Publishing
an imprint of The Quarto Group.
One Triptych Place,
London, SE1 9SH
United Kingdom
T (0)20 7700 6700
www.Quarto.com

EEA Representation, WTS Tax d.o.o., Žanova ulica 3, 4000 Kranj, Slovenia
www.wts-tax.si

Text copyright © 2026 Samantha and Dominic Milner
Photography copyright © 2026 Dan Jones
Design copyright © 2026 Quarto Publishing Plc

Samantha and Dominic Milner asserted their moral rights to be identified as the Authors of this work in accordance with the Copyright Design and Patents Act 1988.

All rights reserved. No part of this book may be reproduced or utilised in any form or by any means, electronic or mechanical, including photocopying, recording or by any information storage and retrieval system, without permission in writing from White Lion Publishing.

Every effort has been made to trace the copyright holders of material quoted in this book. If application is made in writing to the publisher, any omissions will be included in future editions.

A catalogue record for this book is available from the British Library.

HB ISBN 978 1 80570 045 6
PB ISBN 978 1 80570 046 3
Ebook ISBN 978 1 80570 047 0

10 9 8 7 6 5 4 3 2 1

Designer: Georgie Hewitt
Project Editor: Jo Roberts-Miller
Food Photographer: Dan Jones
Appliance Photographer: Alison Field
Food and Prop Stylist: Christina Mackenzie
Food Stylist's Assistant: Sophie Mackinnon
Group Publishing Director: Denise Bates
Senior Editor: Nicky Hill
Senior Designer: Renata Latipova
Senior Production Controller: Rohana Yusef

Printed in Guangdong, China TT/March /2026

Notes

- All calorie counts are per serving where a recipe states 'Serves' or per item when a recipe states 'Makes'
- Metric and imperial measurements are given for all recipes, use one set only and not a mixture of both
- All tablespoons and teaspoons are level
- All milk should be whole/full-fat unless otherwise stated
- All eggs should be UK large eggs or US XL eggs, unless otherwise stated
- Be careful when handling raw chicken, never wash it and never use anything that has come into contact with it, i.e. utensils and chopping boards, on cooked foods, without washing them thoroughly first
- When baking sweet treats, we recommend unsalted butter, and in savoury cooking salted butter. Unless otherwise stated, use butter straight from the fridge
- Do refer to your multicooker manual, as they often operate differently and follow the manufacturer's safety guidelines
- Do not place the multicooker on top of a hot surface/hob/stovetop, or in a heated oven
- Do not place food/liquid in the multicooker when the cooking pot is not inside it. You don't want the heating element to get damaged
- Keep a safe distance away from the multicooker when releasing pressure

CONTENTS

Understanding Mulitcookers 7

Recipe Index by Function 21

Dehydrate 27

Breakfast & Brunch 39

Chicken & Turkey 53

Meat 69

Fish 95

Potatoes 111

Vegetables 127

Soup 139

Pasta & Rice 155

All-in-one Dinners 179

Bread 191

Sweet Treats 205

Index 218

WELCOME

We're Sam and Dom and have been cooking with the slow cooker since 2004, air frying since 2012, added the pressure cooker in 2016, but our world changed in 2020 when we bought our first multicooker.

I was chatting live on BBC Radio just before Christmas and the topic was slow cooker versus air fryer – two very popular kitchen gadgets were going head to head. Because I was often on the radio chatting about our air fryer books, I'm sure they expected me to say air fryer. But, instead, I said I was team multicooker.

There was then a long pause by the radio host . . .

I explained that because I couldn't choose between my kitchen gadget children, I would have to choose the all-in-one.

With a multicooker, I can slow cook then finish the meal using the air fryer, which is perfect if you want to add a pie topping to a stew. I can sauté the beef perfectly to brown the meat first. I can also decide whether I want the food fast – in other words, cooked with the pressure cooker – or slow with the slow cooker function.

Though don't think we will just be covering slow cooking, air frying and pressure cooking because we are also very passionate about the other great multicooker functions. If you love to bake, you will love steam bread, steam bake and steam air fry. Whilst if you love eating healthy, the grill makes the best vegetables and, of course, the steam function is perfect for steaming your fish.

Best of all, it happens in one cooking pot.

In this cookbook (OMG our third!), we are excited to share all the great dishes you can create with one kitchen gadget – you'll see how you can make it work for you, to make mealtimes even easier. But don't worry if you are completely new to the multicooker, we'll start by explaining the basics, then show you how to transform those basics into easy everyday meals that you and your family will love.

SAM & DOM X

UNDERSTANDING MULTICOOKERS

WHAT IS A MULTICOOKER?

A multicooker is a cooking pot that can do several different things. What exactly those things are can vary, as all brands are different. Some multicookers have 3 functions, others have 15. That is why you see models referred to as, for example, the '15 in 1,' where '15' refers to the number of functions. As they are always improving, by the time you read this, perhaps yours will have 20.

The most common multicooker functions are sauté, slow cook, dehydrate, pressure cook, grill/broil and air fry. But they started with a lot less. The first multicooker I remember was an Australian brand and you could only sauté, slow cook, pressure cook and air fry. Nowadays, those 4 settings will be the most common, but there are lots of other new ones included too.

IS AN ELECTRIC PRESSURE COOKER A MULTICOOKER?

I think of electric pressure cookers as the original multicooker. If you own an electric pressure cooker, it might pressure cook, slow cook, sauté, steam, sous vide and have a yoghurt setting. This is one of my electric pressure cookers and it has those 6 settings. It also has presets that you can use, but it's often easier to set your own cooking time. Beyond those settings you also need:

+ and -
This allows you to adjust the cooking time. Even when using a preset, you may still need to adjust the time.

Temperature Up & Down
This takes you from high pressure to low pressure when pressure cooking, along with adjusting the heat level on sauté. Note it's rare in recipes to use low pressure and no recipes in this book use low pressure. When sautéing, an electric pressure cooker gets hot fast. For delicate food, therefore, it's handy to be able to adjust the heat level.

Start & Cancel
Some models start automatically, others require you to press the start button. All have a cancel button. If sautéing, press cancel a couple of minutes early because the cooking pot retains its heat.

Delay Start & Keep Warm
If you don't want to start cooking straight away, there is also a delayed start. Meanwhile, the keep warm setting is ideal if you are not ready to eat straight away. Depending on the brand, your electric pressure cooker or multicooker's keep warm function may keep your cooking pot warm for up to 12 hours.

Recipes in this book that use slow cook, steam, sauté, pressure cook or the yoghurt setting can all be made using an electric pressure cooker.

What About the Air Fryer Lid?
The air fryer lid came about as a quick air fryer solution for pressure cooker owners, but the first versions were poor and came as a separate attachment. You placed

the lid on top of the cooking pot, and it cooked in just one spot so you had to keep turning your food. As Dom says with a smile, 'It made the best toast, though.' It did give other brands the idea of adding an air fryer function, and they made better versions. Without that first air fryer lid, none of the great multicookers we have today would have followed.

What About the Pressure Cooker Lid?
After the air fryer lid came the air fryer basket, which meant it could be an air fryer in its own right. That model of multicooker came with a pressure cooker lid and an air fryer lid. We loved it and that is what the 6 in 1 became. Extra functions were soon added, and our first multicooker like this was the 9 in 1. It could be annoying having to swap the lids, and take two lids with you on road trips.

Two Became One
Brands listened to feedback and they finally designed a multicooker with one lid. All you had to do was press a button or flick a lever, in order to go from one to the other. Brands like to be different, of course, so another one of our favourites has a button to press and looks like a giant can opener.

This is the display of our 15 in 1 that has a slide to switch between groups of functions and one lid.

As well as the features of the original electric pressure cooker, the 15 in 1 can also air fry, grill/broil, steam air fry, steam roast, steam bake, make steam bread, create steam meals, bake, dehydrate, prove dough and it has a built-in probe.

WHAT IF YOU ALREADY HAVE AN AIR FRYER?

Before we bought a multicooker, we were one of the many households that had both an electric pressure cooker and an air fryer. We'd finish food in the air fryer and loved that it had both the low temperature of a dehydrator and the high temperature of a grill/broiler. If this is you, then you can use the air fry, grill and dehydrator settings in your air fryer, and use your electric pressure cooker for almost everything else. If you also have a multicooker like us, you can cook your meat in one gadget, your sides in another, and your dessert in a third!

THE MODERN MULTICOOKERS

In the Milner house, we think of multicookers like mobile phones. When you think of the history of mobile phones (depending on your age), you'll recognise how far they have come. Think of how that first Nokia that sent text messages was the most amazing thing ever! I was 16 when I sent my first text message on my dad's phone. Then came the first camera phone and, wow, technology was incredible. You were so happy with what you had. But, of course, phones got better and better, as new models were released regularly. For many years, I had a phone that was several years behind the latest and was very happy with it, whilst other people might buy the latest on release day. The same applies to multicookers. I still adore my old 2016 multicooker, but I also own the latest version. I'm sure there will be even newer ones soon. It's about looking at the features and deciding which one is right for you. This also means that if you don't need all the bells and whistles, the older 6 in 1 or 9 in 1 can be a frugal way of getting into multicooking, just like you might buy a cheaper air fryer at first, to see if it's for you.

This is the front screen of my 9 in 1. It has just 9 main functions.

It can slow cook, pressure cook, air fry, dehydrate, sauté, grill/broil, bake and roast. Much like mobile phones from 5 years ago, it still works well but it doesn't have all the new features. Also, like mobile phones, brands are different so have different front displays and the buttons aren't all in the same place. I have this problem with two of my electric pressure cookers – they are different models of the same brand and I still use them both. I constantly have to remind myself which one has the sauté button on the bottom left!

With a more budget-friendly 9 in 1, you can follow all the recipes in this book very easily, apart from the steam meals, steam air fry, steam roast, steam bread and steam bake, where you'll have to follow an alternative cooking solution. But the 9 in 1 still provides you lots of great dishes and is a brilliant start to your multicooker journey.

If you are up to date and have the latest multicooker, then you can do it all! See our index on pages 21–25 to find recipes by function.

YOUR MULTICOOKER SETUP EXPLAINED

A common question we get from readers is, 'What should I put inside the cooking pot, and what do the different accessories that come with the multicooker do?' Rory, a reader based in Spain, commented that it's hard to understand which bit is for what purpose.

THE COOKING POT

This is like a saucepan and the shape will vary depending upon the multicooker. The common shape is round and you can remove it from the multicooker, in order to clean it and serve from it, as you would with a slow cooker pot. It should sit securely in the base of your multicooker. They can scratch easily, though, so use wooden spoons and silicone utensils, if you can.

In the pressure cooker world, these are called inner pots, which is a brilliant description, as they are exactly that – the inner pot of your machine.

You can cook directly in your cooking pot, as we do with the prawn curry in a hurry on page 105. However, you can also place one of the following three cooking pot helpers inside, depending on what you are cooking – the metal rack, steamer basket or air fryer basket/crisp plate. But note, you only use one of these at a time.

Demo our cooking pot in action on pages 166-7 with coconut jasmine rice.

THE METAL RACK

This is called a rack but in the early days it was often referred to as a shelf. It's useful in a lot of different recipes. The rack can flip over so you can have it in a high position and use it as a kind of grill, or in a low position when cooking meat. The rack accessory has evolved over time and is now even better. They can vary a lot between multicookers, though. Some have small racks on 1 tier, others have 2 or even 3 tiers. Some racks can be used together, others are available as tall racks, or multiple-tiered racks, which are ideal for dehydrating food. In the early days of multicookers, they were called trivets and were rather small. But because they were compact, it was easy to move the food in and out of the cooking pot.

Demo one of our metal racks in action on pages 170-1 with 'PIP' rice, or on page 29 with banana chips.

When to Use the Metal Rack?
You should use the rack for steam meals, dehydrating, cooking bacon, steak, a whole chicken and most bulky foods. Because it's a rack, though, small foods will fall through the gaps if you don't line it with foil.

THE STEAMER BASKET

There are different types of steamer basket and we like them on stilts, as it gives you height when cooking two things at the same time. The one we use the most spreads out like a flower and expands depending on the quantity of food being cooked.

Demo our steamer basket in action on page 129 with frozen vegetables.

When to Use the Steamer Basket?
Whilst it's called a steamer basket and is most often used when pressure cooking and steaming, it can also be used to cook eggs and mashed potatoes. It's loved by many for the opportunity it gives you to cook one food directly in the cooking pot and another food above. We do this when we cook the potatoes in the steam basket and the meat below for our shepherd's pie on page 85.

THE AIR FRYER BASKET/CRISP PLATE

This piece of equipment will differ depending on the type of multicooker you own. The classic air fryer basket is round and has a 'cook and crisp diffuser,' which clips onto the bottom to give the basket an elevated position. The diffuser clips off for cleaning, which is perfect for getting rid of the grease that collects underneath. Our Speedi has a square cooking pot and a crisp plate that is best described as a grill/broiler insert. It's often called a crisp plate because it became popular as a tool to use when you wanted to crisp up food in the air fryer drawers. If you have a multicooker that looks like a slow cooker, it's likely to have a circular air fryer basket. In our recipes, use whichever comes with your multicooker – an air fryer basket or a crisp plate.

Demo our air fryer basket in action on page 73 with roast pork, or the crisp plate on page 97 with seabass.

When to Use an Air Fryer Basket/Crisp Plate?

Ninety-nine per cent of the time, if you want to air fry, grill/broil, steam air fry or steam roast, you will want to use an air fryer basket or crisp plate. From chips to roast potatoes and apple crumble, using one is your best option. They are also nice and sturdy, which makes them perfect to stack containers onto them.

Did you know, you can also air fry using just the cooking pot and the rack? But note, the food is further away from the heating element when using just the cooking pot or the rack in the lower position, so it can be a little slower when compared to a standard air fryer.

OUR MULTICOOKER ACCESSORIES KIT

Because the multicooker is several gadgets in one, you will need a mix of accessories, some for the air fryer function, another for pressure cooking, and so forth. We have a drawer in our kitchen at home dedicated to our accessories so we can grab them quickly when cooking. We have assumed that your multicooker came with either a regular-sized trivet or a metal rack, an air fryer basket/crisp plate and a steamer basket, as explained on the previous pages.

SILICONE EVERYTHING

Silicone utensils are great because they won't scratch the cooking pot, whilst silicone cake and loaf pans make it easy to turn out the bakes and are quick to clean up.

LARGE SILICONE FREEZER CUBES

Multicookers are perfect for meal prep and making things ahead for the freezer. Many multicooker recipes feed 2–4 and are easy to scale up for bigger families and cooking in bulk. Silicone freezer cubes are the perfect accessory for this. You can pour in leftovers, freeze them, then push the frozen cubes into Ziploc bags to free up your silicone for something else. We use them for preparing meals ahead, storing leftover soup, stock, gravy, stew and even pie filling. They come in different shapes and sizes, so go with the size that best suits your leftovers.

MINI SILICONE FREEZER CUBE TRAYS

These mini cubes look like large ice cube trays and hold 2 tablespoons of liquid. We use them for our yoghurt leftovers, to save some for our next batch (see page 41). They are also great for storing leftover mash. Add a frozen cube of mash to sauces or stews as a brilliant natural thickener.

SPRINGFORM TINS/PANS

Calling all cheesecake fans! The 20cm/8in springform pans are ideal for making cheesecakes, either using the air fryer, pressure cooker or steam bake functions. We also use one in our strata recipe on page 47.

CAKE TINS/PANS

Alongside springform tins/pans, you can also use cake tins/pans, so long as they are made from aluminium, stainless steel, or silicone. We use them for pot in pot rice (see page 170), cooking the protein in a sauce, for cakes and sauces.

RAMEKINS

We love ramekins because they are ceramic, which makes them multicooker safe, but also because their size means they fit in any multicooker.

CERAMICS

Beyond ramekins, you can go large and use any ceramic containers that fit inside your multicooker. We do this with our apple crumble on page 212 or marry me pie on page 56.

GLASSWARE

I can admit it now, I go into IKEA for freezer bags and always leave with yet another collection of glass dishes. In my defence, the small- and medium-sized ones fit perfectly on the rack in the multicooker. They're perfect for freezer meals, batch cooking or reheating leftovers.

OIL SPRAY BOTTLES

Traditionally used with air fryers but so handy for other functions, too. Fill an empty spray bottle with extra virgin olive oil and use it to help make your food crispy. Avoid buying the 1 calorie cooking sprays, as they are watered down and contain ingredients that damage the non-stick properties of the cooking pot.

PUDDING BASINS

If you plan to make steamed puddings, like our jam sponge on page 206, then having a couple of pudding basins is a good option. You could use ceramic, plastic or glass.

TRIVET/COOKING RACK

Depending on the brand of multicooker you are using, the manual will either call this piece of equipment a trivet or a cooking rack. Either way, it's stainless steel and perfect for cooking food in a raised position. You will get one with your multicooker, but we have a drawer full of different trivets, as we find them so useful, and our go-to is what we call a tall trivet. The legs are longer so it's ideal for when you want to cook two different foods at the same time (see our salmon and rice on page 175, or butter chicken and rice on page 172). You can also get them with handles, which makes it very easy to get the food out once cooked.

STACKABLE RACK

We love our stackable, which is like several shelves in one. These were made especially for dehydrated food, so you can stack lots of ingredients in the multicooker at once and make best use of the space.

TWO-TIER RACK

This is also rather popular and is a rack where one shelf clips onto another. It enables you to cook food on two levels at the same time, as you would in an oven, and we use it a lot in the steam meals on pages 180–9.

STEAMER BASKET

I find it useful to have extra steamer baskets – both metal and silicone. You can get so many different ones now, compared to when pressure cooking became popular, and you may find you prefer one style over another. For example, you can get ones that will hold 7 eggs perfectly for making a big batch of egg mayo, or double-stacked steamers for when you want to cook potatoes and veg at the same time.

MEASURING CUPS

I didn't own measuring cups until I bought my first electric pressure cooker, and now I have about three sets! Even though I use metric scales, the cups are ideal for quickly measuring rice, pasta and other grains. Plus, most pressure cooker recipes require 1 cup (240ml/8½fl oz) liquid to go to pressure, and it's much easier to measure this with a cup, than trying to estimate 240ml in a 1-litre jug!

STICK BLENDER

Whether you call it a stick blender or hand-held blender, these are perfect for blitzing or partly blending ingredients in a cooking pot, to create a creamy casserole or soups, homemade gravy or sauces.

MULTICOOKER SPARE PARTS

The two most useful spare parts are spare silicone rings (you never know when it might need replacing) and a spare cooking pot. Just like you'd have more than one saucepan, the same applies with kitchen gadgets. We often cook two things, one straight after the other, and having two pots means we can be getting the other ingredients ready whilst the first cook time is happening. Also, if we have leftovers, sometimes we'll store them in the pot in the fridge, and having a spare pot means you can still use your multicooker.

COOK AND CRISP DIFFUSER

This is the name given to the bottom of the air fryer basket. These diffusers can break, but it is possible to get replacements.

HEAVY-DUTY FREEZER BAGS

We always have plenty of good-quality freezer bags in our kitchen. You can use them for marinating, as well as storing and freezing leftovers. Many of the recipes in this book serve 4, so if you are a 1- or 2-person household, freeze what is leftover. Later in the week, simply tip the frozen meal into the cooking pot and pressure cook for 0 minutes to defrost.

YOUR MULTICOOKER QUESTIONS ANSWERED

Which multicookers have been used in the making of this cookbook?
We surveyed our readers before starting this book and opted for the Ninja Foodi 9 in 1, Ninja Foodi 15 in 1, Ninja Speedi, Instant Pot Duo 7 in 1 multicooker and Instant Pot Duo Crisp. For air fryers with many functions, we also used air fryer flex drawers and air fryer duals.

Help, my multicooker automatically releases pressure!
This is the modern pressure cooker way. A lot of feedback from consumers said they hated having to stand in the kitchen and release pressure themselves. Automatic steam release is the technical name for it, though many refer to it as a delayed release (DR). You can now set a delayed release time when setting the pressure time. It will make a noise when it's ready to release the pressure, so don't get too close to the steam! For the first couple of weeks, though, expect to jump when you hear it, but you soon get used to it.

What if the pressure spits out when releasing?
This happens mainly with starchy foods. A natural pressure release often reduces it. But if it does happen, place a kitchen/tea towel over the pressure release valve and if will soak up the spitting liquid.

My pressure cooker won't go to pressure
This is usually because there is not enough liquid, the liquid was too thick or the sealing ring needs replacing. The sealing ring is easily checked by pressure cooking 4 litres/4.2 quarts cold water for 5 minutes. If it fails to go to pressure, replace your sealing ring. If it isn't the sealing ring, then assess the liquid used – too much passata and other thick liquids will struggle to get to pressure and need to be diluted with stock (see our curry on page 172). Finally, if it looks like it might be the quantity of liquid that's the problem, aim for 1–2 cups (240–480ml/8½–17fl oz) liquid, depending on the size of your cooking pot.

Slow cooker function is way too slow
Some multicookers automatically have the slow cooker function set to low and it can take 10 hours to cook something that would take 3 hours in a classic slow cooker. However, you can increase the temperature! Press the + and adjust to high. Remember, though, since the slow cooker and pressure cooker can be used interchangeably, if the slow cooker is slow and you are panicking that dinner won't be ready, simply switch to pressure cook.

Should you steam air fry or air fry?
As a multicooker has so many different ways to cook a recipe, it can be a case of information overload! If it's a dish that would have a long cooking time in an oven, such as a jacket potato, then steam air fry can be a good option. For foods that require fast cooking, such as onion rings or chicken nuggets, then stick to air fry only. Not only is it quicker but it will help the food be perfectly crisp. So think – food you would roast in an oven rather than cook in a fat fryer are a good fit for steam air fry, but otherwise use air fry.

What about steam bake, roast & bread?
Steam baking and steam roasting produce similar results and can be used interchangeably, depending on your multicooker model. The steam baking, roasting and bread settings all use slower fans so work best for foods that traditionally take longer to cook. The slow fans prevent dishes from over-browning on top – a problem that can occur with air-fried food. The steam roast function works well with food you would traditionally cook in an oven for at least 30 minutes, such as roasted root vegetables, roast chicken, jacket potatoes or even Christmas turkey, whereas I'd use steam bake for cakes and bakes that take less than 30 minutes.

Shout out to the steam bread function
Experimenting with several bread recipes, we found the steam bread function worked much better than air frying, and looked and tasted just like bakery bread.

Steam versus pressure cook
Some multicookers have just one of these functions, so use what you have. They both start by preheating before cooking, but pressure cooking will be faster. In the Milner house, we steam food you associate with steaming (fish and vegetables) and pressure cook the rest. This is partly personal preference but also because when you steam, you don't have to worry about it going to pressure.

Why add cold water & not warm?
When liquid is added to the cooking pot, unless a recipe states otherwise, it should always be cold. The cooking time is based on the time it takes to go to pressure or preheat when steaming. If you use hot water, it would go to pressure more quickly because it would reach boiling point more quickly. The reduced cooking time would result in undercooked food.

Quick versus natural pressure release
'Quick pressure release' means that when it beeps to tell you it's done, you can press cancel and push the valve from sealing to venting, to release the pressure. 'Natural pressure release' means you wait until the pressure has released on its own, then flick it across to venting and you're done. Some recipes call for a bit of both where you wait for a certain number of minutes, then release the pressure. If you're wondering why all recipes are not equal, it's because the food carries on cooking while it's sitting there.

What is 0-minute cook time?
This is popular with pressure cooking. In a nutshell, it means that once the pot has got to pressure, it is done. It is great for quick-cooking food, such as frozen broccoli, parboiling potatoes and warming up leftovers. Other pressure cooking times refer to how long to leave something once it is at pressure.

Can you steam food for 0 minutes?
Technically there isn't the option to do a 0-minute cook time with the steam function. However, you can cheat it. When the multicooker beeps (the beep is loud so you won't miss it) press cancel. This stops the cooking when it has finished preheating. We do this with vegetables that we want to warm up quickly, such as the frozen peas from page 82.

Reducing with bake & air fry
Set the multicooker to bake or air fry at 160°C/320°F if your food is cooked but you feel the liquid needs reducing a bit. Or add the rack and you can warm up your sides in the top position whilst the liquid reduces. Demo with our prawn curry on page 105 or onion soup on page 148.

Why do you season pressure-cooked food after pressure cooking?
When you pressure cook, it reduces the flavours in a dish. If you season first, you'll need to use a lot more seasoning to get the same result. By seasoning at the end, you're avoiding waste.

If you season before pressure cooking or steaming, add more than you think!
This is a good general rule. For example, if you season the butternut squash risotto on page 176 before cooking, use 1 tablespoon dried thyme. If you season it at the end, you'll only need 2 teaspoons.

Which breadcrumbs work best?
You'll notice in some recipes we use golden breadcrumbs (which are the same as Paxo or Shake 'N Bake) and in others we use panko. Golden breadcrumbs are better for when you want a golden colour on the finished dish, such as with scotch eggs on page 91. Panko is better for that perfect crisp, such as with a katsu curry on page 182.

Should I use water, stock or wine?
When steaming or pressure cooking, you need liquid for it to go to pressure. What liquid you use is up to you, but water, stock and wine are our go-to options. You can mix and match these but, please note, if you use water you'll need to season more to compensate.

Help, my cooking pot is dirty & smells
Sometimes you cook something and the food sticks to the bottom, or it might be something with a strong smell. Simply place 480ml/17fl oz/2 cups boiling water, along with 2 teaspoons bicarbonate of soda/baking soda and 1 lemon cut into wedges in the cooking pot. Pressure cook or steam for 20 minutes, followed by a natural pressure release. Rinse out the cooking pot and it'll be like having a brand-new cooking pot again.

THE POPULAR FUNCTIONS OF A MULTICOOKER

I've got a multicooker – which setting should I use? The easiest way to work out what function to use is to think about how you'd cook it without a multicooker. If it's a food you would roast in the oven, then opt for steam roast. If it's something that you would cook in a fat fryer or something you want crispy, then opt for air fry and use the air fryer basket or crisp plate. If it's something you would usually parboil first, or start in the microwave, then opt for steam air fry.

Sauté
One of the main reasons we don't need pots and pans in our kitchen anymore is the sauté function on the multicooker. It's just like using an electric hob/stove. It can take a bit of time to get hot but, once it does, it's very hot. With this in mind, I often add the onion to the pot and wait for the sizzle, rather than just stand over it waiting for it to get hot. I always wait to add the garlic at the last minute, to avoid it cooking too fast and burning in the pot. The sauté setting is ideal for browning onions, making a sauce, stirring already-cooked food to heat through, browning meat and warming up your leftovers.

Air Fry
For many people the air fryer function doesn't need an introduction, as they will have upgraded to a multicooker from owning an air fryer. The air fryer function in a multicooker is just like a typical air fryer; however, it might be a different shape to what you are used to. What we love most, though, is the ability to slow cook a recipe and then finish with air the fryer to add a crispy texture, just like in our lasagne recipe from page 165.

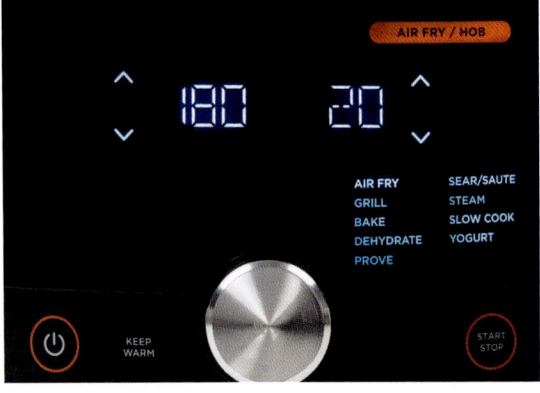

Grill/Broil/Max Crisp
Think of this function as air frying but at a higher temperature. A typical air fryer goes up to 200°C/400°F, whilst the grill/broil setting varies between a low of 210°C/410°F and a high of 240°C/465°F. However, if you have the max crisp function, it usually only cooks at 240°C/465°F. We love our grill/broil function for cooking barbecue-style meat and vegetables, or even toast. The crisp that you can achieve when making toast has us all queuing up in front of the multicooker, impatiently waiting our turn.

Dehydrate
In the same way that you can go high with the grill, you can go low with the dehydrator setting. It's similar to dehydrating with an oven, and is much faster than a traditional dehydrator. On average, food dehydrates in 2–3 hours. Our favourite use of this function is making our own dried herbs (see page 32).

Bake/Roast
Some multicookers have a bake/roast setting, others have them listed separately, and some don't have them at all. In a nutshell, it's air frying but with less power, so it's slower and at a lower temperature. When we experimented with this function, we found we needed a longer cook time – on average an extra 15 per cent more – so we prefer just to use air fry.

Slow Cook
The quality of the slow cooker function in multicookers can vary massively. Some are like for like with your regular slow cooker, others need a much longer cook time. We like to do a test whenever we get a new multicooker and slow cook a simple recipe, such as our cola gammon on page 81, and see if it needs longer, or whether the 'high slow cooking'

setting is really high. Depending on the results, we'll adapt our slow cooker meals in the future. Also note, multicooker slow cooker functions can sometimes be set to a low temperature automatically. If this happens, adjust it to high.

Pressure Cook
Alongside air frying and slow cooking, the pressure cooker is a familiar multicooker function. If you want to cook food fast, then this is the function for you. We love pressure cooking soups and stews but it's also brilliant for cooking vegetables fast, too.

Steam
If you've not steamed yet, it's basically a slower version of pressure cooking and is a great way to ensure food doesn't dry out. In order to steam, the cooking pot needs to preheat to boiling pont, as it does with pressure cooking. Our favourite foods to steam include chicken, fish, vegetables, eggs, Chinese dumplings and, let's not forget, steamed puddings. Whilst the steaming function is common to most multicookers, in modern versions there is also the ability to combine steaming with other great functions.

Steam Air Fry
This function is steaming and air frying at the same time. It's good for food that you are air frying and that has a long cook time. It is not so great for food you want to be crispy, as inevitably the food ends up soggy from the steam.

Steam Bake & Steam Roast
This is a bake/roast version of the steam air fry. In some multicookers, you'll have steam bake or steam roast, and in some you have both, but they can be used interchangeably. We love using this function for roasting meats, roast potatoes and speeding up the cooking time on root vegetables.

Steam Bread
This function will cook your bread like bakery bread. It's light and has the perfect crisp and golden colouring. Try it once and there is no going back. Because the cooking function is partly steam, the bread is cooked in the middle more quickly than it would be without, so there's no need to cook it for longer at a lower temperature, as you would with air frying, which can dry it out.

Steam Meals
This is the multicooker function that brought us all-in-one meals. You can cook the protein part of a meal, as well as the carbs and veg all at the same time. It uses the stacking method, so you don't have to wait around for different parts of the meal to be ready. Plus, all steam meals in this book can be cooked in 10 minutes or less (see pages 180–9).

Yoghurt
This is a great, though specific, function. We use it all the time to create our own homemade yoghurt. On some machines this function is called fermentation.

Prove
This is a great function that takes all the guesswork out of making bread. We combine this with the steam bread function to make bakery-quality homemade loaves.

INGREDIENTS EXPLAINED

TEAM PANTRY

Rice Jasmine rice is our multicooker hero, because it cooks the best. We often have a large bag of jasmine rice, then smaller bags of arborio, for a risotto, and long-grain brown rice for meals with a longer cooking time.

Pasta Dried pasta cooks wonderfully in the multicooker and we always have a good collection – mainly for when Jorge comes home from school starving and asks for pasta for dinner. It's the same cooking time whether you're cooking dried pasta spirals, twists, bows or even spaghetti, which means that when you have bits and bobs of a bag left, you can mix and match.

Beans & Lentils Our favourites are black beans, black-eyed peas, chickpeas and green and red lentils. Red lentils are great for dissolving into sauces, to thicken them naturally and make kids fuller for longer, without them even knowing there are lentils inside.

My Herb Drawer Sofia designed the most amazing herbs and spices drawer for me. If I had to choose my top 10, I'd start with dried basil, dried oregano, dried thyme, dried rosemary, mixed herbs/Italian seasoning, garlic powder, ground ginger, sweet paprika, dried mint and ground cumin.

Salt & Pepper We always have rock salt, as well as your usual salt and pepper grinders. We find that steaming and pressure cooking can dull the flavour, so you need to add more. You'll notice a lot of recipes say season to taste, as we recommend tasting and adding more if you feel it needs it.

Purées, Oils & Pastes I often have a shelf loaded with these extras – garlic, ginger and lemongrass purées, red Thai curry paste, jerk paste, tikka paste and suchlike. I also have a spare bottle of extra virgin olive oil, white wine vinegar, soy sauce, Worcestershire sauce, honey, a quality balsamic vinegar and lemon and lime juice.

FRIDGE & FREEZER FAVOURITES

Cheese, Milk & Eggs We always have milk, eggs and cheese in the fridge – they are our staples. We even store grated cheese in the freezer as a backup.

Vegetables My fridge is always well stocked with my favourite veg. You'll typically find carrots, potatoes, courgettes/zucchini, (bell) peppers and cherry tomatoes in there.

Frozen Vegetables Life can get in the way of even the best-made plans, so I love having frozen veg in the freezer. You'll find frozen cauliflower, broccoli, garden peas, sweetcorn, corn on the cob and sprouts in our freezer. Plus, those small chopped mixed veg bags as they work wonderfully in rice and pasta dishes.

Garlic & Ginger These are so good they deserve an honourable mention. When you sauté, the cooking pot gets hot fast; by using frozen garlic and ginger you slow down the sauté, which helps a lot. Plus, they save you a lot of prep time.

Freezer Cubes My meal planning changed forever when we discovered freezer cubes. They come in various sizes, from a couple of tablespoons to big enough to hold a whole bowl of soup. We've used them for everything from leftover yoghurt, to soup, stock, stews and even pasta bakes.

Poultry, Meat & Fish If there's a deal in the supermarket, I buy it and save it in my freezer for later! These will be a mix of yellow sticker deals, seasonal gluts, or just leftovers. Depending what you're cooking for dinner, you can defrost or cook from frozen.

Leftover Bread We always collect the little bits of bread that don't get used, or buy nice bread when it has a yellow sticker. It's perfect for croutons, as a thickener in soup, or for when you fancy some quick toast. Collect any small bits in a freezer bag.

RECIPE INDEX BY FUNCTION

Not all multicookers are equal and we've created this index so you can quickly find recipes based on the main functions of your multicooker. Recipes are listed under their main function, but may also use other functions in the course of the recipe.

DEHYDRATE

Super Crispy Banana Chips (see page 30)

Dried Fruit Cooking Times (see page 30)

Dehydrated Roast Beef (see page 34)

Greek Beef Jerky (see page 36)

Dried Mushrooms for Stock (see page 32)

Bits & Bobs Dried Herbs (see page 32)

Dried Onion & Garlic (see page 33)

Dried Tomatoes to Purée (see page 33)

2½ Hour Dried Steak (see page 36)

GRILL/BROIL

Ultimate Steak Sharing Tray (see page 92)

Portuguese Pork Kebabs (see page 75)

SAUTÉ

Prawn Curry in a Hurry (see page 105)

Dom's Custard (see page 216)

Creamy Mushroom Sauce for Everything (see page 74)

Dom's Toffee Sauce (see page 208)

Travelling Popcorn (see page 217)

SLOW COOK

Irish Beef Stew & Dumplings (see page 86)

Vegetable Stew with Cheesy Dumplings (see page 136)

Slow-cooked Leek & Potato Soup (see page 151)

SLOW COOK + AIR FRY

Lancashire Hotpot with a Twist (see page 82)

Garlic Bread Topped Lazy Lasagne (see page 165)

PRESSURE COOK

Sunday Dinner Frozen Stock Cubes
(see page 61)

Leftover Pork Cider Casserole
(see page 76)

Must Try Diet Cola Gammon (see page 81)

Leftover Beef Massaman Curry
(see page 88)

Garlic Mussels
(see page 106)

Mixed Seafood Paella (see page 108)

Patatas Bravas Casserole
(see page 124)

A Bag of Frozen Vegetables
(see page 128)

Butternut Squash & Sweet Potato Soup (see page 142)

Creamy Broccoli Cheddar Soup
(see page 145)

My Mum's Super-slimming Chunky Soup
(see page 146)

Big Batch Bacon & Lentil Soup
(see page 152)

Quick Pasta for Any Occasion
(see page 157)

Kitchen Cupboard Pasta Bake
(see page 160)

Date Night Spaghetti & Meatballs
(see page 162)

Coconut Lime Jasmine Rice (see page 166)

Salsa Chicken Rice Box (see page 168)

Vegetable Rice
(see page 171)

Creamy Butter Chicken & Yellow Rice (see page 172)

Marinated Salmon & Vegetable Rice
(see page 175)

Kyle's Butternut Squash Risotto (see page 176)

Classic Jam Spong Pudding (see page 206)

Dom's Sticky Toffee Pudding (see page 208)

Jazzy Apple Sauce (see page 74)

Bubble & Squeak (see page 120)

Mustard Mash (see page 120)

Root Vegetable Mash (see page 121)

Cauliflower Mash (see page 121)

Creamed Cabbage & Leeks (see page 130)

No-prep Creamy Vegetable Soup (see page 141)

Taco Mixed Bean Soup (see page 152)

'Pot in Pot' White Rice (see page 170)

AIR FRY

Nut-free Autumn Granola (see page 43)

Bacon Sandwiches on the Rack (see page 48)

Chicken Kyiv, Chips & Garlic Butter Peas (see page 62)

Cheddar Cheese Chicken Thighs (see page 66)

Garlic Parmesan Chicken Wings (see page 66)

Pork & Apple Burgers (see page 78)

20-minute Lemon Pepper Fish Goujons (see page 103)

Dom's Cheesy Potato Cakes (see page 123)

Easy Garlic & Rosemary Focaccia (see page 197)

Garlic Bread Croutons (see page 201)

Tear & Share Cheesy Garlic Bread (see page 203)

Quick Bifanas (see page 75)

10-Minute Texas Toast (see page 201)

PRESSURE COOK + AIR FRY

Jorge's Baked Beans on Toast (see page 50)

Paprika Roast Chicken (see page 54)

Marry Me Family Chicken Pie (see page 56)

Simply the Best Turkey Crown (see page 59)

Shepherd's Pie with Meaty Mash (see page 85)

Rosemary & Thyme Scotch Eggs (see page 91)

Prawn & Halloumi Orzotto (see page 100)

Garlic & Herb Roast Potatoes (see page 117)

Egg Mayo & Cress Jacket Potatoes (see page 118)

Honey Glazed Parsnips (see page 134)

PROVE

YOGHURT

20-minute French Onion Soup (see page 148)

Sofia's BLT Pasta Salad Jars (see page 158)

Dom's Bread Dough for Everything (see page 192)

Overnight Creamy Yoghurt (see page 40)

Make-ahead Yoghurt (see page 40)

STEAM

Mushroom & Asparagus Baked Eggs (see page 44)

5-minute Spiced Seabass (see page 96)

Dom's Quick Steamed Eggs (see page 44)

Creamy Wilted Spinach (see page 130)

STEAM MEALS

Vietnamese-style Steak Noodle Bowls (see page 180)

Chicken Katsu Curry with Sushi Rice (see page 182)

10-minute Moroccan-spiced Lamb Steaks (see page 185)

Maple Ginger Salmon Packets (see page 186)

Caribbean Summer Veg with Rice & Peas (see page 188)

STEAM AIR FRY

Barbecue Chicken Drumsticks & Corn (see page 64)

Steam Air Fry Chips (see page 113)

Crispy Curried Kale (see page 131) and **Asparagus Bundles Wrapped in Bacon** (see page 133)

Back to Childhood Apple Crumble (see page 212)

Claire's Concrete Cake (see page 214)

STEAM ROAST

Make-ahead Mediterranean Strata (see page 47)

Steam Roasted Pork & Crackling (see page 73)

Broccoli-crusted Salmon (see page 98)

Fennel & Thyme Hasselback Carrots (see page 133)

Garlic Roasted Fennel (see page 131)

STEAM BREAD

Irish Soda Bread Minis (see page 198)

Weeknight Beer Bread (see page 194)

STEAM BAKE

Peri Peri Sweet Potato Wedges (see page 114)

Easiest-ever Biscoff Cheesecake (see page 210)

HOW TO DEHYDRATE

Until we got an air fryer, we had never considered dehydrating food ourselves. It had just never entered our heads. Then, here we were with an air fryer that we had bought off one of the TV shopping channels, which had a dehydrator setting, and for the first time ever we were considering it.

We bought every fruit we could think of and dehydrated it all, and it was a huge success. Then we tried fresh herbs, making use of leftovers, then came meat. It was great fun and tasted pretty good, too.

That was back in 2019, and it was the only air fryer with a dehydrator setting at the time, but now most of them have one. Then, all-in-one multicookers added a dehydrator setting, too. In this chapter, we will be running through all our favourite foods to dehydrate, starting with, of course, fruit.

It doesn't take long to get the food ready to dehydrate, then all you have to do is leave the multicooker to it. Once it beeps, store the dehydrated food in your favourite airtight containers – yes, a use at last for all that Tupperware you bought!

WHY DEHYDRATE?

Dried food is an amazing way to preserve foods. Look at your fruit bowl – any fruit that the kids nagged you to buy but haven't eaten and is now just going to be left for a few weeks, then thrown in the bin – dehydrate! Make dried apple and pear chips for the kids' lunch boxes or as a snack on a road trip. Any fruits that have the same dehydrating time can be done together.

One food that is often heavily wasted is fresh herbs. You follow a recipe that needs a handful of fresh mint and then you have half a bag left. That half a bag, along with the other half a bag of basil, thyme, rosemary and such like, can be dried, then stored in jars.

Aside from preventing food waste, dehydrated food tastes delicious, and will often be made when the food is at its best.

TOP TIPS

Cooking Time When dehydrating food, it often has a long cooking time as it takes place at a low temperature. Think of it as a slow cooker. If you want banana chips for an evening snack, then put them on in the early afternoon. However, when dehydrating whole berries, do it the day before, so you are not rushing.

Season First If you are seasoning dried food, do it before dehydrating. That way, the seasoning adds a flavoursome base and makes a real difference. We like to sprinkle cinnamon on our apple chips.

Oil You can add a couple of sprays of olive oil for extra crispiness on dehydrated fruit and veg. With meat, spraying olive oil helps the texture once cooked.

Sweetener Adding a little stevia can enhance the sweetness, especially when dehydrating strawberries and bananas. But, of course, it's optional.

Dehydrator Stack We love having the stackable dehydrator accessory for our multicooker (see opposite and page 15), as we can dry a lot more fruit and veg or herbs at once. If you don't have one, use your air fryer basket/crisp plate or the tiered racks.

Cooking Temp We have found that the sweet spot for the perfect dehydrated food is 60°C/140°F.

Mandolin We love our mandolin and, when you want thinly sliced fruit and veg for the dehydrator, using one is the easiest way. Shop around but be careful – it's so easy to hurt yourself.

SUPER-CRISPY BANANA CHIPS

Banana chips are one of those super-easy recipes that has you thinking, 'How can something that tastes so good be so easy?!' Simply coat thinly sliced bananas in lemon juice, load them onto the rack, place them in the multicooker and, like magic, come back later to perfect banana chips.

SERVES **4**
FUNCTIONS **DEHYDRATE**
PREP **10 MINUTES**
DEHYDRATOR TIME **3 HOURS**
TOTAL COOK TIME **3 HOURS**
CALORIES **70**

2 large bananas
120ml/4fl oz/½ cup lemon juice
Extra virgin olive oil spray
½ tsp stevia powder (optional)

01 Peel, then cut the bananas into thin slices with a mandolin. Place the slices into a bowl with the lemon juice and toss gently, making sure they don't break.

02 Using a dessertspoon, carefully load the banana slices onto the air fryer basket/crisp plate of your cooking pot, or dehydrator stack, if you have one. Make sure none of them are overlapping. Spray the slices with olive oil and sprinkle with stevia, if using.

03 Press dehydrate and dry for 3 hours at 60°C/140°F, or until completely dried and crispy.

DRIED FRUIT COOKING TIMES

ALL AT 60°C/140°F

Strawberry chips – 2 hours
Pear chips – 2 hours
Apple chips – 2 hours
Whole raspberries – 9 hours
Whole blueberries – 16 hours
Whole blackberries – 16 hours
Whole grapes – 54 hours
Orange slices – 3 hours
Lemon and lime slices – 2 hours

THE 54-HOUR RAISIN

Yes, that is not a typo. It takes 54 hours using the dehydrator setting to transform whole juicy seedless grapes into raisins. They taste better than shop-bought raisins, though they are larger in size. I don't like the idea of leaving my kitchen gadgets running overnight so we did this during hours we were awake at home and it took us a few days, but they tasted so good and were well worth the wait. We presented them to Sofia, who is fussy and says she hates raisins but loves grapes, and she couldn't believe how they looked and refused to try them. But Jorge loves raisins and ate them all in one sitting!

DRIED MUSHROOMS FOR STOCK

Chefs rate dried mushrooms as the best stock ingredient.

MAKES **1 HERB JAR**
FUNCTIONS **DEHYDRATE**
PREP **8 MINUTES**
DEHYDRATOR TIME **2 HOURS**
TOTAL COOK TIME **2 HOURS**
CALORIES **24**

115g/4oz mushrooms

01 Carefully cut the mushrooms into thin slices. Spread them out in the air fryer basket/crisp plate in the cooking pot.

02 Press dehydrate and dry for 2 hours at 60°C/140°F, or until completely dried.

03 If you want them chopped into smaller bits, transfer the mushrooms to a food processor or blender and chop, or place them whole in an airtight container for later. If you are chopping them into smaller bits, you can store them in a herb jar.

BITS & BOBS DRIED MIXED HERBS

Drying herbs is one of my favourite ways to use the dehydrator, if not my favourite. Just think how often you add dried herbs to a recipe you're making - they are so useful. Mixed herbs, or Italian seasoning as it is known in the US, feature in most of the dishes I make. In this recipe, we show you how to make your own from fresh herbs. You can mix and match, choosing your favourites, to create your own dried herb mix.

MAKES **½ HERB JAR**
FUNCTIONS **DEHYDRATE**
PREP **8 MINUTES**
DEHYDRATOR TIME **3 HOURS**
TOTAL COOK TIME **3 HOURS**
CALORIES **20**

10g/¼oz fresh basil
10g/¼oz fresh oregano
7g/⅕oz fresh thyme
3g/½₀oz fresh flat-leaf or curly parsley

01 Clean the fresh herbs, keeping any stalks on, and pat them dry with kitchen/paper towel. Place all the herbs in the air fryer basket/crisp plate inside the cooking pot.

02 Press dehydrate and dry for 3 hours at 60°C/140°F, or until completely dried.

03 Remove the stalks (it is much easier to do this now) and transfer the leaves to a food processor or blender. Pulse to make your preferred size of dried herbs.

MIXED HERBS 101

Rosemary & Thyme Shop-bought dried versions of these two herbs can be problematic – they're so big you can get them stuck in your teeth! But dehydrate your own, and you can make them as small or as big as you like. Blitz the rosemary in a food processor or blender and make it as small as dried basil.

Flavour Up the Oregano If you often add oregano to your recipes but feel as though you need to add lots to get the flavour, opt for a less finely chopped finish when you pulse it in your food processor or blender.

Mixed Herbs If you're making your own mixed herb selection, we recommend using 28–30g (about 1oz). This will make enough to fill half a small herb jar. Make it in batches if you want more.

DRIED ONION & GARLIC FOR EVERYTHING

We use onion and garlic in most recipes but we often have odds and ends left over that can go to waste. When you're drying onion and garlic, you can do a batch of just onion or just garlic, or a mix of the two, as they have the same cooking time.

MAKES **1 HERB JAR**
FUNCTIONS **DEHYDRATE**
PREP **10 MINUTES**
DEHYDRATOR TIME **3 HOURS**
TOTAL COOK TIME **3 HOURS**
CALORIES **98**

1 medium brown onion
1 garlic bulb

01 Peel and thinly slice the onion and the garlic. Place them in the air fryer basket/crisp plate inside the cooking pot.

02 Press dehydrate and dry for 3 hours at 60°C/140°F, or until completely dried.

03 Remove the garlic and onion, then transfer to the food processor or blender. Pulse to make a dried onion and garlic mix, then store in a herb jar for later.

DRIED TOMATOES TO TOMATO PURÉE

This is an interesting concept and a tasty one, too. You dry out tomatoes using your dehydrator, then add just the right amount of water to make tomato purée, or paste as you might call it. You could also add the dried tomatoes to your herb or spice mix.

MAKES **1 JAR**
FUNCTIONS **DEHYDRATE**
PREP **8 MINUTES**
DEHYDRATOR TIME **3 HOURS**
TOTAL COOK TIME **3 HOURS**
CALORIES **113**

4 medium tomatoes
1 tsp dried oregano

01 Thinly slice the tomatoes and place in a single layer on the air fryer basket/crisp plate of your cooking pot. Sprinkle with the oregano and season with salt and pepper.

02 Press dehydrate and dry for 3 hours at 60°C/140°F, or until completely dried.

03 Remove the tomatoes and place in a food processor or blender. Pulse to make dried tomato powder.

04 To turn the powder into tomato purée/paste, mix 1 teaspoon of tomato powder with 1½ teaspoons cold water. Use it in your cooking as you would shop-bought tomato purée.

Did You Know? In classic peri peri recipes, dried tomato powder is one of the key ingredients. Next time you have a peri peri fakeaway, get your tomato powder out of the kitchen cupboard.

DEHYDRATED ROAST BEEF

Back in 2023, some people upgraded their air fryer to include a dehydrator setting just for this roast beef recipe! Others were concerned that dehydrating beef meant drying it out. The reality is that dehydrated beef is the same as cooking it slowly in the air fryer. It crisps the beef as it slow cooks. Get ready for the most tender roast beef - it is well worth the wait.

SERVES **6**
FUNCTIONS **DEHYDRATE**
PREP **5 MINUTES**
DEHYDRATOR TIME **7 HOURS**
TOTAL COOK TIME **7 HOURS**
CALORIES **234**

1.1kg/2lb 7oz topside/top round roast beef
1 tbsp extra virgin olive oil
1 tbsp dried thyme

01 Smother the beef with olive oil and give it a generous seasoning on all sides with salt and pepper. Sprinkle with the dried thyme, then place the beef on the air fryer basket/crisp plate of the cooking pot.

02 Press dehydrate and dry for 7 hours at 60°C/140°F, turning halfway through, or until it reaches an internal temperature of 55°C/130°F or above.

03 When the multicooker beeps, remove the beef and wrap it in foil. Leave to rest for 30 minutes before slicing.

Make Your Roast Beef a Meal We love our sides with our roast beef and serve it with shop-bought Yorkshire puddings, roast potatoes from page 117, gravy and mixed vegetables.

- **Yorkshire Puddings (Chilled)** - 2 minutes air fry 180°C/360°F
- **Yorkshire Puddings (Frozen)** - 3 minutes air fry 180°C/360°F
- **Mixed Country Vegetables** - 0 minute steam
- **Reheating Gravy** - 5 minutes air fry 180°C/360°F

Brisket Wins When you think of brisket, your mind automatically imagines slow cooking, otherwise it's like trying to chew rubber. But dehydrated brisket is an 'OMG that's good' moment.; it's so tender, you could swap topside for rolled brisket. If your brisket is not rolled, ask your butcher to do it for you. This method of cooking is ideal for those who love a medium-rare beef, because the dehydrate is slow cooking but also air crisping at the same time.

What About Silverside? What Britains and Australians call silverside is very similar to the joint used in the US to make corned beef. Instead of making beef jerky with it (see page 36), you can cook it whole as above. For our readers who make corned beef and cabbage for St Patrick's Day, why not use this as your corned beef recipe and serve it with our creamy cabbage on page 130?

GREEK BEEF JERKY

SERVES **8**
FUNCTIONS **DEHYDRATE**
PREP **15 MINUTES**
MARINATING TIME **OVERNIGHT**
DEHYDRATOR TIME **6½ HOURS**
TOTAL COOK TIME **6½ HOURS**
CALORIES **323**

....

1.1kg/2lb 7oz silverside/bottom round beef

GREEK MARINADE
2 tsp garlic purée
1 tbsp balsamic vinegar
1 tbsp lemon juice
1 tbsp extra virgin olive oil
2 tsp Greek yoghurt
2 tsp dried oregano

01 Add all the Greek marinade ingredients to a bowl and mix well.

02 Slice the silverside as thinly as you can, with the grain not against. Place the slices in the bowl with the marinade and give it a really good mix. Cover with cling film/plastic wrap and leave to marinate in the fridge overnight.

03 The next day, spread out the marinated beef strips in the air fryer basket/crisp plate of your cooking pot. Press dehydrate and dry at 60°C/140°F for 6½ hours, turning halfway through with tongs.

Beyond the Greek We have used our favourite Greek marinade for this recipe. We like this because the yoghurt helps prevent the beef jerky from being overly tough and gives it a lovely flavour. But, of course, you could use any favourite marinade, avoiding ones with sticky ingredients that go dark or hard when cooking, such as honey, barbecue sauce or maple syrup.

THE 2½ HOUR DRIED STEAK

When I think of steak, I always think of 4 minutes on each side in the air fryer. But you can dehydrate a steak in 2½ hours and you'll be surprised at its taste and texture – it is like a cross between a steak and jerky.

....

SERVES **1**
FUNCTIONS **DEHYDRATE**
PREP **5 MINUTES**
DEHYDRATOR TIME **2½ HOURS**
TOTAL COOK TIME **2½ HOURS**
CALORIES **421**

....

1 x 225g/8oz ribeye steak
1 tbsp extra virgin olive oil
1 tbsp dried steak seasoning

01 Smoother the steak with olive oil, then give it a generous seasoning on all sides with salt and pepper. Sprinkle with dried steak seasoning, then place the steak in the air fryer basket/crisp plate of the cooking pot.

02 Press the dehydrate button and dry for 2½ hours at 60°C/140°F, turning halfway through with tongs, or until the steak reaches an internal temperature of 55°C/130°F or above, depending on how you like it.

03 When the multicooker beeps, remove the steak and wrap it in foil. Leave to rest for 30 minutes before slicing.

04 Slice the steak into 1cm/½in – or even thinner – slices.

BREAKFAST & BRUNCH

OVERNIGHT CREAMY YOGHURT

If you have a yoghurt button on your multicooker, then you can use it to make your own yoghurt. It'll be the best yoghurt you've ever tried and, trust us, you won't want to go back to shop-bought yoghurt ever again. The creamy texture of this yoghurt is so thick, it compares to crème fraîche or that incredibly thick Greek yoghurt you get when visiting a Greek restaurant.

....

SERVES 4
FUNCTIONS PRESSURE COOK, YOGHURT
PREP 15 MINUTES
PRESSURE COOK TIME 2 MINUTES
YOGHURT COOK TIME 8 HOURS
TOTAL COOK TIME 8 HOURS 2 MINUTES
CALORIES 250

....

- 2 heaped tbsp yoghurt with active cultures (we use thick Greek yoghurt)
- 1.9 litres/64fl oz/8 cups UHT/fairlife/long-life milk (we use semi-skimmed/2%)
- 1 tbsp vanilla extract (optional)

01 Pour 3 litres/3⅛ quarts water into the cooking pot. Secure the pressure cooker lid, set the valve to sealing and pressure cook for 2 minutes, followed by a quick pressure release. (This will sterilise the pot before making the yoghurt.) This will take a good 10 minutes to get to pressure.

02 When you've released the pressure, carefully pour out the water – it will be hot. (You could use it for washing up!) Make sure no water remains in the pot.

03 Scoop the yoghurt into the cooking pot along with 240ml/8½fl oz/1 cup milk. Whisk until well mixed and starting to froth.

04 Pour in the rest of the milk and whisk until frothy like in a coffee shop.

05 Secure the lid on the multicooker (no need to set to sealing). Press the yogurt setting and set the time to 8 hour, then press start. (With some multicookers you may need to press yoghurt, then press the arrow down to fermentation and set the time to 8 hours.)

06 When you're yawning and ready for bed, and the multicooker has beeped, remove the cooking pot from the multicooker, and make sure you don't stir. Cover with a silicone lid or tightly wrap the top in foil and place the pot in the fridge for 8 hours to chill.

07 When you wake up in the morning, remove the cooking pot from the fridge and set up your straining system. Place a colander over a bowl, then cover the colander with kitchen/paper towel.

08 Gradually pour the yoghurt over the kitchen/paper towel, a little bit at a time. Now, go and get ready for the day. Come back in about 1 hour, once it has strained through the kitchen/paper towel and into the bowl.

09 Repeat until all the yoghurt is strained. (It may take between 2 to 3 rounds of straining to do a full batch; if you have a large strainer, it will be less.) You now have lovely creamy yoghurt. Stir in vanilla extract, if using, and enjoy.

Make-ahead Yoghurt Reserve 2 heaped tablespoons of yoghurt in an ice cube tray and keep them in the freezer. When you next want to make yoghurt, defrost and use these. You won't have to buy active culture yoghurt each time you make yoghurt, as you will have created your own!

TOP TIPS

Quality We have found that the creamy, full-fat or luxurious yoghurts work best. If you are using low-fat yoghurts, follow our scoop tip below.

Scoops For perfect, creamy yoghurt, we use 2 heaped scoops of yoghurt. We tried 3, but found that was only necessary if you are using a low-fat variety.

Active Cultures It's the active cultures that successfully make the yoghurt, so when choosing what yoghurt to use as a base, look on the packaging to make sure it contains them.

Milk You should use UHT, or long-life milk, when making yoghurt. They don't have to be stored in the fridge, which is helpful if you plan to make lots. Plus, UHT milk doesn't need to be boiled first.

Settings Firstly, we sterilise the cooking pot before making the yoghurt. This is done with the pressure cook button. After this we press yoghurt, or on some machines it's called fermentation.

PLAN YOUR YOGHURT SCHEDULE

Because yoghurt takes more than 16 hours from start to finish, we've found the best system is to incorporate it into your bedtime routine. If you do, you'll have the yoghurt straining in time for breakfast. The straining will most likely have to be done in batches, but the first batch will be ready for 8am. We've based this on an 11pm bedtime.

2.30pm Sterilise the cooking pot

2.45pm Prepare the ingredients

3.00pm Start making the yoghurt

11.00pm Transfer the yoghurt from the multicooker to the fridge

7.00am Remove the cooking pot from the fridge and strain the yoghurt

8.00am Yoghurt is ready for breakfast

NUT-FREE AUTUMN GRANOLA

The big benefit for us as multicooker owners is that we have all these different functions on one machine and can mix and match. Whilst we are waiting for the yoghurt to finish straining, we can make a big batch of granola. This is perfect for storing in your favourite airtight container and ideal to keep for busy weekday mornings. Serve it with your yoghurt for breakfast.

Autumn is my favourite foodie season, so this is loaded with apple sauce, pumpkin spice, cranberries and maple syrup.

....

SERVES **4**
FUNCTIONS **AIR FRY**
PREP **8 MINUTES**
AIR FRY COOK TIME **8 MINUTES**
TOTAL COOK TIME **8 MINUTES**
CALORIES **346**

....

- 90g/3¼oz/1 cup porridge oats/rolled oats
- 35g/1¼oz/¼ cup sunflower seeds
- 28g/1oz/¼ cup pumpkin seeds
- 1 tsp ground ginger
- 1 tsp ground cinnamon
- 2 tsp pumpkin spice
- 2 tsp apple sauce
- 2 tsp vanilla extract
- 1 tbsp extra virgin olive oil
- 2 tbsp maple syrup
- 20g/¾oz/¼ cup coconut flakes
- 40g/1½oz/¼ cup dried apricots, finely chopped
- 28g/1oz/¼ cup dried cranberries
- 55g/2oz/¼ cup raisins or dates (or a mix of both)

01 Add all the ingredients to the cooking pot, apart from the coconut flakes, apricots, cranberries and raisins or dates. Give it a good stir with a wooden spoon.

02 Secure the air fryer lid on the multicooker, set the temperature to 180°C/360°F and the cooking time to 6 minutes.

03 When it beeps, stir in the coconut flakes, apricots, cranberries and raisins. Cook for 2 more minutes at the same temperature to warm them up, or until toasted enough to your liking.

04 Divide between four yoghurt-filled bowls and serve with fresh fruit, or store in meal-prep jars to take to work.

Overnight Oats Transform your granola supplies into overnight oats. Mix 3 tablespoons of water with 200g/7oz homemade yoghurt in a jar (we use Mason jars, as on page 158). Stir in 1 teaspoon vanilla extract and ½ teaspoon each of dried ginger and pumpkin spice. Set aside half of the yoghut mixture for later. Sprinkle 200g/7oz oats, 28g/1oz finely chopped apricots and 28g/1oz finely chopped cranberries into the jar, then spoon the reserved yoghurt on top. Decorate with a few more pieces of chopped fruit, then cover with a lid. Store in the fridge overnight for breakfast on the go.

Make-ahead Prep Tip Because granola uses a few different pantry staples, it can feel like an effort to prep them on a busy morning. What I do is I prep all the dry ingredients (minus the dried fruit) – multiplied by 5 – and place them in a storage jar. I give it a really good shake, then the next time I want to make granola, I just add a fifth of the jar to the cooking pot with the wet ingredients. It makes life so much easier.

DOM'S QUICK STEAMED EGGS

Dom often has these for breakfast, and they are the multicooker version of poached eggs.

SERVES **1**
FUNCTIONS **STEAM**
PREP **2 MINUTES**
STEAM COOK TIME **2 MINUTES**
TOTAL COOK TIME **2 MINUTES**
CALORIES **235**

2 large eggs
Extra virgin olive oil spray

01 Place 240ml/8½fl oz/1 cup water into the cooking pot. Pull out the legs of the crisp plate and then lower it into the cooking pot. It will then be in a high position. Alternatively, if using the rack, flip it over into the high position.

02 Place a side plate on the crisp plate/rack and spray it with a little olive oil to stop the eggs from sticking. Crack 2 eggs onto the plate before placing the lid down on the steamer. Press steam and cook for 2 minutes (if the eggs are close to the steamer vent, they take 2 minutes; if they are in the bottom position, they take 4–5 minutes).

03 When the steamer beeps, remove the plate carefully with oven gloves and serve.

Pressure Cooker Opt for a 0-minute cooking time with QPR.

One Egg or Two? Follow the same method and cook time for 1 or 2 eggs!

MUSHROOM & ASPARAGUS BAKED EGGS

Grab your favourite ramekins and take your steamed eggs to the next level.

SERVES **2**
FUNCTIONS **AIR FRY, STEAM**
PREP **5 MINUTES**
AIR FRY COOK TIME **8 MINUTES**
STEAM COOK TIME **4 MINUTES**
TOTAL COOK TIME **12 MINUTES**
CALORIES **598**

170g/6oz button mushrooms
4 asparagus spears
¼ medium red onion
2 tbsp salted butter
1 tbsp roughly chopped fresh basil
1 tsp garlic powder
1½ tsp smoked paprika
4 tbsp crème fraîche
28g/1oz/⅓ cup grated Parmesan
Extra virgin olive oil spray
2 large eggs

01 Quarter the mushrooms, if they are large, chop the asparagus into 2.5cm/1in chunks, and peel and finely chop the onion. Place all the veg into the cooking pot, add the butter and press air fry. Set the temperature to 180°C/360°F and air fry for 8 minutes.

02 Check the asparagus is fork tender and add a couple of extra minutes if it's not quite there. Stir in the basil, garlic powder, paprika and a generous seasoning of salt and pepper. Pour in the crème fraîche, then sprinkle in the grated Parmesan. Give it another good stir – it will be a beautiful colour from the paprika and nice and creamy.

03 Grease two ramekins with olive oil spray, then divide the mixture between them. Create a little hole in the middle of each and crack an egg into the gap.

04 Add 240ml/8½fl oz/1 cup water to the cooking pot. (No need to clean it first as the steam will help make it easier to clean after cooking.) Add the air fryer basket/crisp plate, then carefully add the ramekins. Press steam and cook for 4 minutes. After the steam cooking time you will have perfect baked eggs.

Air Fry & Steam The mushrooms, asparagus and red onion are air fried first, then mixed with cheese, cream and paprika to make a creamy veg base. Finally, an egg is cooked on top for the perfect Mediterranean breakfast.

MAKE-AHEAD MEDITERRANEAN STRATA

If you have not heard of a strata, then imagine a frittata with leftover bread. It is cooked in a springform tin/pan so has a cake look. The egg and cream mixture soaks into the bread and you can include your favourite frittata fillings, too. When you cut into your finished strata, it has a custardy texture and is perfect for lazy Sunday mornings, or why not have it for Christmas or Easter breakfast?

....

SERVES **6**
FUNCTIONS **SAUTÉ, STEAM ROAST**
PREP **8 MINUTES**
SAUTÉ COOK TIME **5 MINUTES**
STEAM ROAST COOK TIME **40 MINUTES**
TOTAL COOK TIME **45 MINUTES**
CALORIES **436**

....

½ medium red onion
140g/5oz chorizo
170g/6oz cherry tomatoes
1 x 30g/1oz bag fresh basil
1 tbsp sun-dried tomato paste
1 tbsp garlic purée
125g/4½oz French bread stick
4 large eggs
4 tsp crème fraîche
1 tbsp dried oregano
1 tbsp smoked paprika
115g/4oz/1 cup grated Gouda cheese
55g/2oz/½ cup grated mature/sharp Cheddar
Extra virgin olive oil spray

BALSAMIC SALAD
¼ Little Gem lettuce
55g/2oz cherry tomatoes
Handful fresh basil leaves
Handful rocket/arugula
1 tbsp balsamic vinegar

01 Peel and slice the onion and slice the chorizo, then add them to the cooking pot. Press sauté and when you hear the sizzle, give it a stir with a wooden spoon and sauté until the onion has softened and the chorizo is getting some colour.

02 Press cancel on the sauté and stir in the cherry tomatoes. Roughly chop the fresh basil and add three-quarters of it to the pot with the sun-dried tomato paste and garlic purée. Chop the bread into 2cm/¾in chunks and add them to the pot, too. Stir well (you want the bread to be well coated in the mixture). Set aside while you make the batter.

03 Crack the eggs into a large mixing bowl. Beat with a dessertspoon, then gradually add the crème fraîche, remaining basil, the oregano and smoked paprika. Add the grated cheeses to the bowl with a generous seasoning of salt and pepper. Mix well.

04 Tip the bread mixture from the cooking pot into the bowl with the eggs and continue to mix well, making sure the bread is coated well in the flavoured batter.

05 Grease a leakproof springform tin/pan, then pour in the egg and bread mixture. Add 240ml/8½fl oz/1 cup water to the cooking pot. (Use a wooden spoon to scrape any bits stuck on to the side. Steaming the strata will help clean this for you.) Add a trivet/rack to the cooking pot and cover the springform pan with foil before lowering onto the trivet/rack. Set to steam roast and cook for 35 minutes at 180°C/360°F, or until a thermometer almost comes out clean or reads 65°C/150°F or above. Remove the foil and cook for a further 5 minutes uncovered.

06 Remove the trivet/rack and the springform tin/pan and set aside to cool for 10 minutes. Release the springform and slice the strata into portions.

07 We love to serve our strata with some roughly chopped Little Gem lettuce, cherry tomatoes, basil leaves, rocket/arugula and a drizzle of balsamic vinegar.

Make The Night Before If we are having this for breakfast or brunch, we will make it up to the point of steam roasting the night before, then finish it in the morning. Preparing ahead also means the ingredients soak into the bread a lot more.

Reheat Your Strata Add a medium slice to your air fryer basket and air fry at 160°C/320°F for 4 minutes.

BACON SANDWICHES ON THE RACK

Bacon cooked to your liking, loaded into sourdough bread and cooked on the rack is a favourite among multicooker users. Instead of placing the bacon in a single layer on the rack, you position it as if you are hanging out your laundry without any pegs. It creates a fantastic crisp to your bacon, and you will want to do this again and again.

SERVES **4**
FUNCTIONS **AIR FRY**
PREP **4 MINUTES**
AIR FRY COOK TIME **9 MINUTES**
TOTAL COOK TIME **9 MINUTES**
CALORIES **580**

8 rashers back bacon/lean bacon
Butter, for spreading
8 slices thick sourdough bread
4 tsp tomato ketchup (optional)

01 Line the bottom of the cooking pot with foil. We recommend moulding the foil into the shape of your multicooker. Place the rack at its highest position.

02 Hang the bacon from the rails of the rack, like you would hang out your clothing if you had no pegs. Spread the rashers out so they don't overlap, to get an even cook.

03 Add the air fryer lid and set the temperature to 200°C/400°F. For just-cooked bacon, cook for 7 minutes, for a medium cook, choose 9 minutes, or if you love really crispy bacon, select 12 minutes. Meanwhile, spread butter on the slices of bread.

04 When the air fryer beeps, use oven gloves to remove the rack from the cooking pot. (That way it will be so much easier to grab the bacon.)

05 Using tongs, place 2 slices of bacon on half the slices of bread, then drizzle over tomato ketchup, if using, and top with another slice of buttered bread. Serve warm.

BACK BACON COOKING TIMES

Just-cooked – 7 minutes
Medium – 9 minutes
Super-crispy/well-done – 12 minutes

STREAKY/AMERICAN BACON COOKING TIMES

Just-cooked – 9 minutes
Medium – 11 minutes
Super-crispy/well-done – 14 minutes

JORGE'S BAKED BEANS ON TOAST

Jorge's favourite breakfast is baked beans on toast and when we are staying at a hotel, he will always have it, regardless of the other delicious smells. We thought he would love it if we made him his own. This baked bean recipe is perfect for two adults and two children, and makes a filling, cheap breakfast, or breakfast for dinner, as they say.

....

SERVES **4**
FUNCTIONS **PRESSURE COOK, SAUTÉ, AIR FRY**
PREP **4 MINUTES**
PRESSURE COOK TIME **35 MINUTES**
SAUTÉ TIME **5 MINUTES**
AIR FRYER COOK TIME **3 MINUTES**
TOTAL COOK TIME **43 MINUTES**
CALORIES **366**

....

170g/6oz/1 cup dried haricot beans
480ml/17fl oz/2 cups vegetable stock
250g/9oz/1 cup passata
2 tbsp Worcestershire sauce
4 tbsp barbecue relish
1 tbsp granulated sugar

TO SERVE
12 mini slices soda bread (see page 198), or 4 regular slices bread
4 tsp butter
Mature/sharp Cheddar, grated (optional)

01 Pour the beans and the stock into the cooking pot. Secure the lid on the pressure cooker, set the valve to sealing and pressure cook for 35 minutes, followed by a quick pressure release.

02 After releasing the pressure, drain the remaining liquid from the beans and set the pressure cooker to sauté.

03 Add the passata, Worcestershire sauce, barbecue sauce and sugar, season generously with salt and pepper, and stir. Add more passata, if you prefer saucier baked beans.

04 Cancel sauté and carefully place the rack/crisp plate in the top position over the beans. Arrange the bread on the rack/crisp plate (in batches of 2–4 slices, depending on the size of your multicooker). Set the temperature to 200°C/400°F and air fry for 3 minutes, or 4 for a crispier toast.

05 Spread butter on the toast and pour the baked beans over the top. Sprinkle with some grated cheese, if using, before serving.

Prefer Barbecue Baked Beans? Swap the passata for your favourite barbecue sauce instead.

Cheese & Bean Toasties Instead of serving your beans over toast, why not make cheese and bean toasties? Cut 4 slices of bread and spread butter on one side of each. Place 2 slices side by side and butter-side down in the air fryer basket/crisp plate in the top position. Spoon 2 tablespoons beans and 1 tablespoon grated cheese over each slice, then place aother slice of bread on top. Press the bread down to stop it from flying off whilst cooking, set the temperature to 240°C/465°F and grill/broil for 4 minutes.

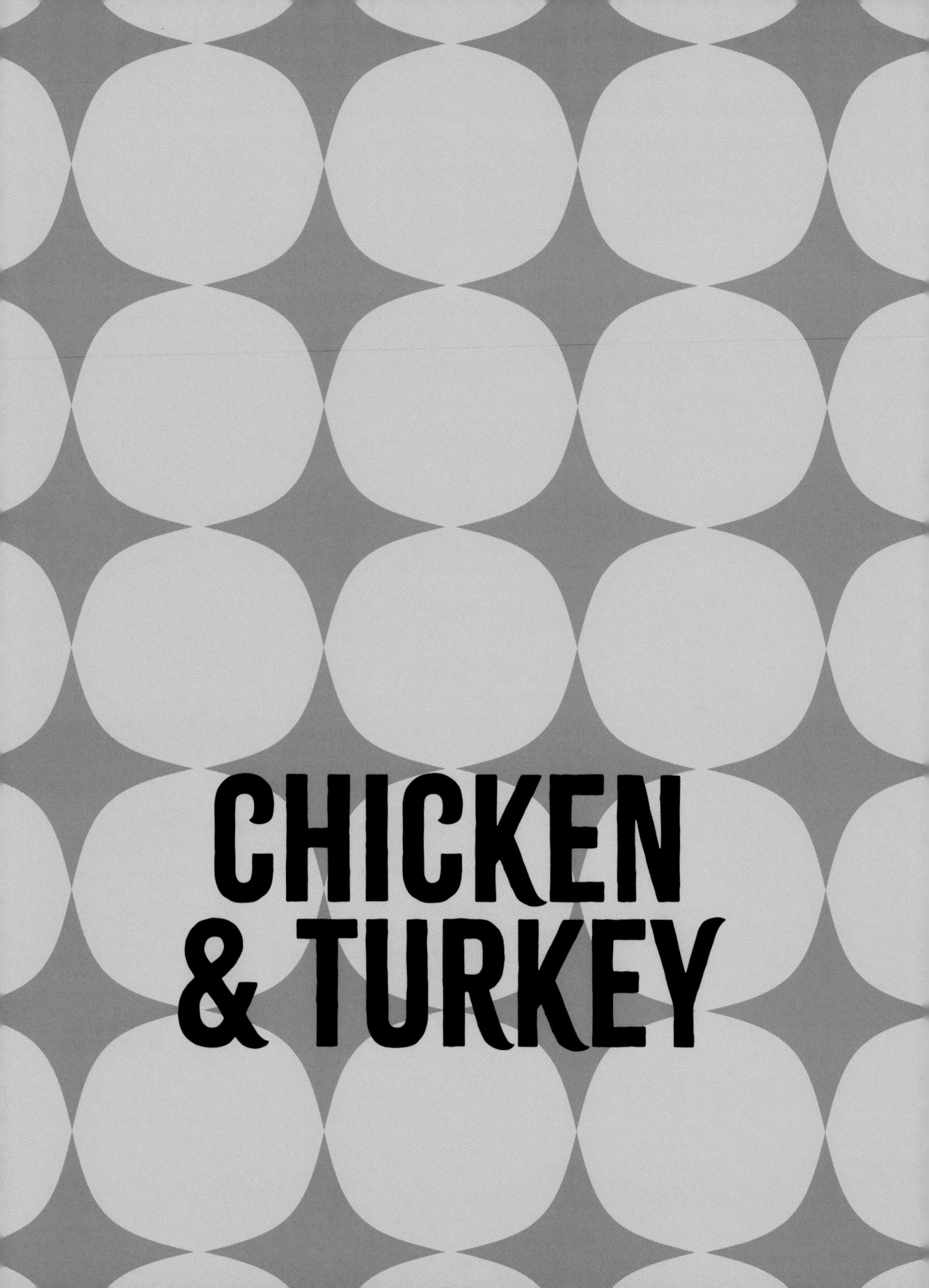
CHICKEN & TURKEY

HOW TO MULTICOOK A WHOLE CHICKEN

Most air fryer, pressure cooker and slow cooker users will name a whole chicken as one of their favourite foods to cook. I would say that the same goes for us. But why? Because, you don't have to waste time adding butter under the skin, they cook a lot faster than in a conventional oven, and there's no need to preheat the oven, so you can get it going more quickly for dinner. Most importantly, though, the finished product is so much moister than an oven-roast chicken.

PAPRIKA ROAST CHICKEN

Smoked paprika, garlic mayonnaise, lemon juice and sun-dried tomato paste make a delicious marinade for your chicken.

SERVES **4**
FUNCTIONS **PRESSURE COOK, AIR FRY**
PREP **5 MINUTES**
MARINATING TIME **1 HOUR**
PRESSURE COOK TIME **12 MINUTES**
AIR FRY COOK TIME **17 MINUTES**
TOTAL COOK TIME **29 MINUTES**
CALORIES **896**

1.8kg/4lb whole chicken
240ml/8½fl oz/1 cup vegetable stock or water

PAPRIKA MARINADE
3 heaped tbsp garlic mayonnaise (we use aioli)
2 tbsp lemon juice
2 tbsp extra virgin olive oil
2 heaped tbsp smoked paprika
2 tsp sun-dried tomato paste

01 To make the paprika marinade, place the mayonnaise in a mixing bowl, then gradually add all the other ingredients. Mix with a fork until combined. Remove a quarter of the marinade and set aside in a small bowl for later.

02 Place the chicken on a dinner plate. Then, using your hands, smother the whole chicken with the marinade on all sides, then place the chicken on a plate in the fridge to marinate for 1 hour.

03 Pour the stock or water into the bottom of the cooking pot, then set the air fryer basket/crisp plate in place.

04 Arrange the chicken on the air fryer basket/crisp plate, breast-side up, and make sure it is pushed down and is not going to move about during the cooking process. (If you are not using an air fryer basket, you will need to tie the chicken legs up with string so the chicken doesn't move about too much.)

05 Secure the lid on the multicooker, set the valve to sealing, and pressure cook for 12 minutes, followed by a 5-minute natural pressure release. After releasing, remove the lid. The internal temperature of the chicken should read approximately 55°C/130°F. (See our cooking time notes opposite, if you plan to cook with just the pressure cooker.)

06 Using a pastry brush, brush the top and sides of the chicken with the reserved marinade – basically brush any bits you can reach without removing it from the multicooker. Swap the pressure cooker lid for the air fryer lid (if you have that type of multicooker) because it's time to air fry. Press air fry and cook at 180°C/360°F for 17 minutes, or until crispy to your liking and an internal temperature of 70°C/160°F or above. Leave to rest for about 15 minutes before serving.

BUT, HANG ON A MINUTE, YOU HAVE A MULTICOOKER WHICH MEANS YOU HAVE CHOICES...

You could air fry, steam air fry, steam roast, slow cook, pressure cook, or even start with air fry and then pressure cook or vice versa, and the list goes on. What we've done above is share the step-by-step pictures of the original multicooker method of pressure cook and air fry, then we include different times and temperatures for the various options (see below).

MULTICOOKER CHICKEN COOKING TIMES

Pressure Cooker Only Don't swap to the air fryer lid, if you want a quick, pulled-chicken-style texture. For a large chicken, i.e. 1.8kg/4lb, cook the chicken, breast-side down (to make it juicy and tender), for 24 minutes in total plus a 5-minute natural pressure release.

Air Fry Only Cook for a total of 50 minutes at 180°C/360°F. Start cooking the chicken breast-side down for 30 minutes, then flip over, re-apply the marinade and cook for a final 20 minutes.

Slow Cook For a juicy whole chicken we find that slow cooking for 3½ hours is perfect. If you have a multicooker that runs at a lower temperature on its slow cooker setting, then we recommend 4 hours, but do an internal temperature check.

Steam Air Fry & Steam Roast We found that the steam roast looked more golden, like a traditional oven-baked chicken, whereas, the steam air fry was a little paler. Both steam air fry and steam roast take about the same amount of time as air fry only at the same temperature.

Cooking with a Probe If you have a multicooker with a built-in probe, you can place the probe in the thickest part of the chicken, set it to the chicken setting of 75°C/165°F and, when it reaches 75°C/165°F, it will stop cooking. If you are steam roasting, it usually takes 50 minutes but when we added the probe it was exactly 48 minutes.

MARRY ME FAMILY CHICKEN PIE

The craze of the last few years has been 'marry me chicken' – chicken cooked in a creamy paprika and sun-dried tomato sauce that's so good it'll get you a marriage proposal, or so they say. This is our family version; we made one for Mum and Dad, and another smaller one for the kids, and served them with buttery green beans!

SERVES **4**
FUNCTIONS **PRESSURE COOK, SAUTÉ, AIR FRY**
PREP **10 MINUTES**
PRESSURE COOK TIME **4 MINUTES**
SAUTÉ COOK TIME **10 MINUTES**
AIR FRY COOK TIME **12 MINUTES**
TOTAL COOK TIME **26 MINUTES**
CALORIES **1475**

About 350g/12oz leftover roast chicken
2 large white potatoes
2 large carrots
240ml/8½fl oz/1 cup vegetable stock
1 large red onion
1 tbsp extra virgin olive oil
120ml/4fl oz/½ cup red wine
6 sun-dried tomatoes
2 tbsp garlic purée
2 heaped tbsp mayonnaise
2 heaped tbsp smoked paprika
2 heaped tbsp mixed herbs/Italian seasoning
55g/2oz/⅔ cup grated Parmesan
1 × 150g/5½oz pack garlic and herb cream cheese (we use Boursin)
240ml/8½fl oz/1 cup double/heavy/thickened cream
1 × 320g/11oz sheet ready-rolled puff pastry
Egg wash

01 To prepare the chicken, either shred a full chicken leg, or a mixture of bone-in chicken and breast chopped into chunks.

02 Peel and cut the potatoes and carrots into 2cm/¾in cubes. Pour the stock into the cooking pot and set the steamer basket in place. Add the potatoes and carrots, secure the pressure cooker lid, set the valve to sealing and pressure cook for 4 minutes, followed by a quick pressure release.

03 Remove the potatoes and carrots and set them aside. Pour the leftover stock into a bowl to use later. Press sauté on the multicooker. Peel and thinly slice the onion and add it to the cooking pot with the olive oil. Wait for the sizzle, then stir the onion until it has changed colour and is nice and soft. Without pressing cancel, pour the stock back in, and the red wine to deglaze the cooking pot. Scrape up any bits that are stuck to the bottom.

04 Thinly slice the sun-dried tomatoes and add them to the pot with the garlic purée, mayonnaise, paprika, mixed herbs, grated cheese and a generous seasoning of salt and pepper. Give it a good stir. Add the cream cheese and cream, and continue to stir until well mixed and starting to thicken.

05 Return the chicken, potatoes and carrots to the pot, and stir to mix well. If you feel the sauce is not thick enough, blend a few of the potatoes and carrots with a stick blender (they make an amazing thickener). After one last stir, cancel sauté, transfer the mixture to small pie dishes that will fit in the multicooker. (We use two – one for the adults and one for the kids.)

06 Open the ready-rolled puff pastry and use the parchment attached to it as a work surface. Using a cutter, cut out heart shapes until you run out of pastry. Decorate the tops of the pies with the hearts, overlapping them to create a heart-shaped topping, and brush the surface with egg wash. (At this point, you could transfer them to the fridge, until needed.)

07 Clean the cooking pot, put the air fryer basket/crisp plate into the multicooker and place one pie at a time on the air fryer basket/crisp plate. Press air fry and set the temperature to 180°C/360°F. Cook for 12 minutes, or until the pastry is golden and the filling has an internal temperature of 70°C/160°F or above. Repeat with the remaining pies. (The cooked pies will hold their heat, so it's a recipe that is easy to prepare in batches.)

Freezer Pie To freeze the pies for another day, let the sauce cool before adding the chicken, potatoes and carrots. Transfer the mixture into pie dishes and top with the heart-shaped pastry, and freeze before cooking. Defrost the pies, then cook them in the air fryer at 180°C/360°F for 20 minutes.

Quick Trick Avoid having to add the mayonnaise, garlic purée, paprika and mixed herbs separately for the sauce, by saving 2 heaped tablespoons of the marinade used for the paprika chicken on page 54 and using that instead.

SIMPLY THE BEST TURKEY CROWN

This is our famous turkey recipe that gets kitchen gadget owners talking every Christmas. It is magically moist and the breast skin is incredibly crispy, because we do the best of both worlds – pressure cook, to keep the turkey moist, *and* just before the end of the cooking time we air fry it for a crispy skin.

SERVES **6-8**
FUNCTIONS **SAUTÉ, PRESSURE COOK, AIR FRY**
PREP **10 MINUTES**
SAUTÉ COOK TIME **8 MINUTES**
PRESSURE COOK TIME **35 MINUTES**
AIR FRY COOK TIME **10 MINUTES**
TOTAL COOK TIME **53 MINUTES**
CALORIES **950-705**

3kg/6½lb turkey crown/bone-in turkey breast (giblets removed and discarded)
Extra virgin olive oil spray
2 tsp dried mixed herbs/Italian seasoning

HIDDEN VEG GRAVY
1 medium brown onion
3 medium carrots
2 medium white potatoes
4 celery sticks
2 tbsp extra virgin olive oil
240ml/8½fl oz/1 cup dry white wine
480ml/17fl oz/2 cups turkey stock, or any poultry stock
1 tsp dried thyme

01 We love to make a hidden veg gravy to go with our turkey crown, made of root vegetables and some of the turkey and juices. As this is sautéed first, we are starting here. Peel and finely chop the onion, peel and chop the carrots and potatoes into 1cm/½in chunks, and trim and chop the celery into 1cm/½in chunks. Place all the prepared vegetables in the cooking pot, along with the olive oil. Press sauté and when you hear the sizzle, get out the wooden spoon and start stirring. Sauté until the onion has softened.

02 Cancel the sauté and deglaze the cooking pot with the wine and stock. Give it a good stir to get rid of any bits that are stuck to the bottom and sides.

03 Arrange the turkey directly over the vegetables, breast-side up. Secure the pressure cooker lid, set the valve to sealing and cook for 35 minutes, followed by a 5-minute natural pressure release. (If using the probe, insert the probe at the thickest part of the breast and set it manually to 60°C/140°F, and it will stop when it reaches that temperature.)

04 After releasing the pressure, give the turkey breast a good spray with olive oil and a generous seasoning with salt and pepper, as well as the mixed herbs. Press air fry and cook at 200°C/400°F for 10 minutes, or until crispy to your liking, and it has an internal temperature of 70°C/160°F or above.

05 Carefully remove the turkey from the cooking pot and set aside to rest.

06 Let the stock and vegetables at the bottom of the pot cool a bit. Shred the turkey from the wings, as it flavours turkey gravy so well, then use a stick blender to blitz everything together. Season the gravy generously to taste with salt, pepper and the dried thyme, and serve with your turkey.

Calculate Your Turkey Bone-in poultry takes 6 minutes per 450g/1lb to cook when pressure cooked, plus the 5-minute natural pressure release. We take 5 minutes off the pressure cook time to finish in the air fryer. So, if you have a 2kg/4lb 8oz turkey it will take 27 minutes to pressure cook or 22 minutes if pressure cooking and air frying.

The Size of Your Pot We can just fit a 3kg/6lb 8oz turkey in our cooking pot. Try to keep the weight of the turkey at this level, or it will be too close to the heating element and will burn on top.

Fridge Turkey The best thing about turkey cooked this way is that it stays moist for much longer. There'll be no dry turkey sandwiches and leftovers are very versatile – you could use them for our curry on page 88. or our pie on page 56.

Extra Veg We served our turkey with broccolini and sprouts. Whilst the turkey is resting, steam your veg. For broccolini, we recommend 10 minutes, but keep the sprouts in for an extra 5 minutes after that. We also thawed shop-bought cauliflower cheese and steam baked for 15–18 minutes at 180°C/360°F.

SUNDAY DINNER FROZEN STOCK CUBES

One thing I cook a lot using the pressure cooker function is stock. I have made everything from beef, lamb, pork, vegetable and fish stock, and they all make the food in the pressure cooker taste even better. But the best time to make stock is during the prep for a Sunday roast dinner, as you can use up so many bits as you cook. That way, it doesn't feel as if you are making any effort. As you eat the roast, you can be pressure cooking your stock. Then just drain it as you do the washing up!

MAKES **8**
FUNCTIONS **SAUTÉ, PRESSURE COOK**
PREP **8 MINUTES**
SAUTÉ COOK TIME **10 MINUTES**
PRESSURE COOK TIME **25 MINUTES**
TOTAL COOK TIME **35 MINUTES**
CALORIES **290**

1 tbsp extra virgin olive oil
1 medium brown onion
4 medium carrots
4 celery sticks
1 large leek
1 garlic bulb
480ml/17fl oz/2 cups dry white wine
700g (1lb 9oz) veg or veg peelings
  (we use a mixture of potatoes, carrots, parsnips and cabbage)
Handful fresh herbs (we use parsley, thyme and rosemary)
8 black peppercorns

01 Press sauté on your cooking pot, set to low and drizzle in the olive oil. Peel and roughly chop the onion, peel and slice the carrots, and trim and slice the celery and leek. (Save the celery ends and the onion skin to add later.) Add the vegetables to the cooking pot.

02 After sautéing for about 5 minutes, peel the garlic cloves and stir them in. Deglaze the pot with the white wine. Don't cancel sauté, though, as the vegetables will continue to cook with the wine. Sauté for another 5 minutes, then press cancel.

03 Add in any other vegetable scraps you have, such as the skin from the onion, the celery ends and have a good poke around in your fridge. Have you got any old vegetables that need using up? You could add some spring/green onions, an old carrot, some fennel or cabbage that never got used because you had a takeaway instead. Pour in 1.4 litres/6 cups cold water and give it a stir. Cover with the fresh herbs. I always aim for a good handful, and you can mix it up by using fresh parsley, thyme or rosemary. No need to chop them – just throw the herbs in the cooking pot. Finally, add the whole peppercorns and it's ready to go.

04 Secure the pressure cooker lid on to the multicooker, set the valve to sealing and pressure cook for 25 minutes. Follow with a quick pressure release.

05 After releasing the remaining pressure, remove the lid. Pour everything through a mesh strainer over a big bowl to catch the stock. Let it sit for a little while, to get all the last bits of liquid through. You can do this in batches, if you have made a lot of stock or your strainer is too small. You now have vegetable stock. I recommend pouring it into freezer cubes and, once completely cool, freezing for another day. You can cook the freezer cubes from frozen, in other pressure cooker recipes; they will have defrosted by the time the food goes to pressure. They also add delicious flavour to your multicooker recipes.

What Does Your Sunday Dinner Look Like? I have based the ingredients for this Sunday dinner stock on items that are easy to mix and match. You could make it with the leftover sides you've served with a roast dinner, or simplify things.

Customise for Meat & Fish Halve the amount of leftover scraps and add beef bones, pork bones, or the chicken or turkey carcass instead. Place these on top of the veg, before adding the water, and you will make a meaty stock. If you want to make a fish stock, use leftover scraps of uncooked fish, or the bones from when you have filleted fish – it all works well. Just don't skip using a mesh strainer afterwards because you don't want any tiny bones sneaking into your stock.

CHICKEN KYIV, CHIPS & GARLIC BUTTER PEAS

Chicken Kyiv with its garlic butter filling and crispy breading, is an air fryer dream come true. Add homemade Cajun chips and garlic butter peas, and you are in comfort food heaven. To stop that delicious garlic butter leaking out, we create a basil and cream cheese barrier.

....

SERVES **2**
FUNCTIONS **AIR FRY**
PREP **12 MINUTES**
AIR FRY COOK TIME **46 MINUTES**
TOTAL COOK TIME **46 MINUTES**
CALORIES **579**

....

1 tbsp salted butter
2 heaped tsp cream cheese (we use Philadelphia Light)
1 large garlic clove
1 tsp dried parsley
1 × portion chips (see page 113)
2 medium boneless, skinless chicken breasts
4 basil leaves
70g/2½oz/½ cup plain/all-purpose flour
2 large eggs, beaten
40g/1½oz/¾ cup golden breadcrumbs (we use Paxo)
160g/5¾oz/1 cup frozen garden peas

01 Start by making the garlic butter. In a mixing bowl, add three-quarters of the butter and the cream cheese. Mince the garlic and add this, along with the dried parsley and some salt and pepper. Give it a good mix with a fork and then wrap it tightly like a sausage in cling film/plastic wrap and place in the freezer for 30–60 minutes. While the garlic butter is chilling, you can start on the chips.

02 Cook the chips in the air fryer basket/crisp plate of the cooking pot until they are 6 minutes away from the end of their cooking time (20 minutes), then set aside. (We will finish the process after cooking the Kyivs.)

03 Place the chicken breasts on a clean chopping board and slice into the top of the breast at an angle (this stops the garlic butter from squirting out later). Scoop out and discard about a teaspoon of the chicken breast to create a hole, making sure the top of the breast still covers the hole like a lid.

04 Remove the garlic butter from the freezer and place a heaped teaspoon of garlic butter onto a basil leaf, then top with it with another basil leaf and squash it down, as if you're making a basil sandwich. Place this basil sandwich in the hole in the chicken breast, making sure it is covered by the flap of chicken. Repeat with the other breast.

05 Now it's time to bread your chicken Kyivs. Place the flour in one shallow bowl, the beaten eggs in another and the breadcrumbs in a third. Carefully dip the stuffed chicken breast in the flour, then drench in the egg and finish in the breadcrumbs. As you do this, be careful that the breast does not open to reveal the secret garlic butter and basil sandwich, as you want to keep that filling inside.

06 Place the chicken Kyivs in the air fryer basket/crisp plate and cook on air fry for 20 minutes at 180°C/360°F. Remove from the multicooker and set aside.

07 Place the frozen peas in a ramekin, add the remaining garlic butter and some salt and pepper, and place on one side of the air fryer basket/crisp plate. Add the almost-cooked chips to the other side and cook them together for 6 minutes at 180°C/360°F.

08 Serve the chips and peas with your chicken Kyivs.

Love Spice? We doubled the Cajun seasoning for a delicious, spicy spin on classic chips.

Garlic Butter Peas The first time we tried this, we found that after making the garlic butter filling for the chicken Kyiv, we had just over a teaspoon of the filling left, so we cooked some peas with this and it was delicious!

BARBECUE CHICKEN DRUMSTICKS & CORN

One of the best things to cook in the air fryer are chicken drumsticks. They taste amazing and my favourite way to cook them is in a sticky sauce. We've used pantry staples in this recipe to make a delicious Korean-inspired barbecue sauce, which we use to marinate, cook and serve with the drumsticks. And, of course, drumsticks are perfect with corn on the cob.

SERVES **4**
FUNCTIONS **STEAM AIR FRY**
PREP **10 MINUTES**
MARINATING TIME **2 HOURS**
STEAM AIR FRY COOK TIME **32 MINUTES**
TOTAL COOK TIME **32 MINUTES**
CALORIES **615**

1kg/2¼lb chicken drumsticks
6 corn on the cobettes

KOREAN-STYLE BARBECUE MARINADE
300ml/10fl oz/1¼ cups barbecue sauce (we use Bullseye)
2 tbsp frozen chopped ginger
1 tbsp frozen chopped garlic
2 tsp soy sauce
1 tbsp rice vinegar
100g/3½oz/½ cup soft brown sugar
1 tsp crushed dried chilli flakes (to taste)
4 tsp clear honey
2 tsp finely chopped pickled red jalapeños (to taste)

01 In a large bowl, combine all the barbecue marinade ingredients and mix well. Set about 3 heaped tablespoons of the marinade aside in a small bowl – this is perfect for adding to the chicken and the corn once cooked.

02 Place the chicken drumsticks in the large bowl with the marinade. Cut the cobs in half, then add them, too. Mix everything well to coat in the marinade. Cover the bowl in cling film/plastic wrap and leave in the fridge to marinate for a minimum of 2 hours, or overnight. (These are ideal for making dinner ahead.)

03 When you are ready to cook the chicken and corn, remove the cling film and place the chicken drumsticks in a foil tray or a paper liner. (You don't want your multicooker to get dirty with this barbecue sauce! We love to use 18cm/7in square foil trays.) Spoon over some of the marinade from the large bowl, so that you get as much of that lovely flavour on the chicken as possible. Depending on the size of your multicooker, you may need to cook them in batches.

04 Pour 240ml/8½fl oz/1 cup water into the cooking pot, then add the air fryer basket/crisp plate. Place the foil tray inside and set it to steam air fry at 180°C/360°F for 20 minutes. Halfway through the cooking time, turn the chicken over with tongs for an even cook. Meanwhile, get another foil tray ready with the corn, so that when the chicken is done, the corn can go straight in.

05 When the multicooker beeps, check the chicken has an internal temperature of 70°C/160°F or above, before you swap it for the corn. Check there is enough water in the cooking pot. If not, adjust it to the original 240ml/8½fl oz/1 cup. Most of the time I find it has used half the liquid, so I just need to add half again. Once you have added your foil tray of corn, steam air fry at 180°C/360°F for 12 minutes.

06 Serve the chicken and corn in paper-lined baskets for a real barbecue vibe, with wipes to hand for the sticky fingers. Use a pastry brush to coat some of the reserved marinade over the chicken and corn before serving.

Just the Korean-style Sauce If you are licking your lips thinking about other foods you would love to serve with this sauce, then do just that. We have separated the ingredients, to make this easier to do.

Air Fry Only If you don't have the steam air fry option, air fry without the liquid at the same temperature for 22 minutes for the chicken drumsticks and 15 minutes for the corn on the cobs.

CHEDDAR CHEESE CHICKEN THIGHS

SERVES **4**
FUNCTIONS **AIR FRY**
PREP **10 MINUTES**
AIR FRY COOK TIME **25 MINUTES**
TOTAL COOK TIME **25 MINUTES**
CALORIES **659**

....

1kg/2¼lb bone-in chicken thighs
2 tsp dried chives
180g/6¼oz cheese biscuits (we use Cheddars)
70g/2½oz/½ cup plain/all-purpose flour
2 large eggs

01 Season the chicken thighs well with salt, pepper and the dried chives.

02 Use a food processor or blender to turn the cheese biscuits into crumbs, or tip them into a plastic bag and bash them with a rolling pin.

03 Place the flour in a shallow bowl, crack the eggs into another, and the biscuit crumbs in a third. Beat the eggs with a fork. Coat the chicken thighs in the flour, then drench them in the egg, finally coat thoroughly in the biscuit crumbs.

04 Place the breaded thighs in a single layer in the air fryer basket/crisp plate inside the cooking pot. You may have to do this in batches. Press air fry and cook at 180°C/360°F for 25 minutes, or until the thickest part of the chicken reaches an internal temperature of 70°C/160°F or above.

05 Serve with a sour cream and chive dip, and barbecue sauce.

GARLIC PARMESAN CHICKEN WINGS

SERVES **4**
FUNCTIONS **STEAM AIR FRY, AIR FRY**
PREP **8 MINUTES**
STEAM AIR FRY COOK TIME **15 MINUTES**
AIR FRY COOK TIME **13 MINUTES**
TOTAL COOK TIME **28 MINUTES**
CALORIES **671**

....

1kg/2¼lb chicken wings
2 tbsp extra virgin olive oil
¼ tsp garlic powder
¼ tsp onion powder
1 tbsp dried oregano
1 tbsp smoked paprika

GARLIC PARMESAN COATING
115g/4oz/½ cup salted butter
2 tsp garlic purée
2 tbsp roughly chopped curly parsley
55g/2oz/⅔ cup grated Parmesan

01 Place the chicken wings in a large bowl and season well with salt and pepper. Pour in the olive oil and mix well with your hands (add the oil first as it acts like a glue for the seasoning to stick to the chicken). After a hand wash, sprinkle in the garlic, onion, oregano and smoked paprika powders, mixing well with your hands for a thorough coating.

02 Add 240ml/8½fl oz/1 cup water to the cooking pot, then place the air fryer basket/crisp plate inside. Arrange the chicken wings in the air fryer basket/crisp plate. Spread them out or cook them in batches. Press steam air fry and cook at 180°C/360°F for 15 minutes (or 18 minutes if just air frying). When the multicooker beeps, tip the wings out into a clean bowl.

03 Cut the butter into chunks, place in a ramekin and squeeze in the garlic purée. Place the ramekin in the air fryer at 120°C/250°F and press air fry or bake (if your air fryer doesn't go this low) for 5 minutes to melt the butter.

04 Remove the garlic butter, add the parsley and Parmesan, and stir.

05 Pour this mixture over the chicken wings and use a wooden spoon to make sure they are thoroughly coated. Place the chicken wings back in the air fryer basket/crisp plate in a single layer. Air fry for 8 minutes at 200°C/400°F. (If there is some yummy garlic Parmesan coating at the bottom of the bowl, use a pastry brush to brush this over the wings, too.)

MEAT

HOW TO STEAM ROAST WITH THE PROBE

Nowadays, multicookers have so many different settings. At first there was just pressure cooking, air frying and slow cooking, as the golden ways to cook your Sunday roast, but now we have steam roast, along with a probe to get that perfect internal temperature.

As I love roast pork, especially if there is some crispy crackling, I thought I would show you how to cook any roasting meat using the steam roast setting, demonstrating with pork loin. Once you know how, you can step it up a level and repeat with roast chicken, beef, lamb or any other favourite meat.

TOP TIPS

Probe or Not to Probe The probe is only available with newer multicookers, but, if you have one, make use of it, as it makes roasting so much easier (see box on the right for more information).

Crackling Here in the UK, we love our pork crackling, which is made by cooking the fat on the pork. But if crackling is not your thing, follow this recipe and just ignore the crackling bits.

Marinated Pork Talking about crackling, if you marinate pork with the crackling, it's very easy to blacken it. Instead, rub the marinade on the fat-free areas instead.

Don't Have a Steam Roast Setting? You can cook roast pork using the air fryer setting instead. After 45 minutes do an internal temperature check to see how far along it is. Depending on what size pork joint you are cooking, we find the air fryer takes between 45–60 minutes.

All Tied Up Because of the air circulation from multicookers, it's recommended that you tie your meat up. Whether that is with some string around the pork loin to keep it in place, or tying up the legs of a whole chicken, it makes cooking much more even.

THE BUILT-IN PROBE

If you have a multicooker with a built-in probe, it's a great feature to use. How it works is that it is inserted into the fattest part of the food you are cooking for the best reading. Then, instead of setting the time and temperature to cook, you press probe and set your desired internal temperature. It will stop cooking as soon as it reaches that temperature. You can keep an eye on the temperature to get an idea of how far along you are. We timed it when we cooked several roast dinners using steam roast to see how long the probe took and these were the results

- **1.8kg/4lb large whole chicken** – 48 minutes
- **1.3kg/3lb gammon/ham** – 1 hour 16 minutes
- **1kg/2lb 4oz lamb shoulder** – 55 minutes (cooked to medium)
- **1.3kg/3lb topside/round roast beef** – 32 minutes (cooked to medium-rare)

Fillet Steak/Filet Mignon on the Probe You can also grill your steak using the probe. Place the probe into the thickest part of the steak at an angle (so it doesn't go all the way through) and season it with salt, pepper and steak seasoning. Press grill and set the probe to 50°C/120°F. When it's done, you'll have perfect medium rare steak.

DO YOU HAVE LEFTOVERS?

Here in the Milner house, we love our leftovers and the delicious meals we can make from them. Here are some ideas on how to use your leftover roast dinner staples

- Marry me chicken pie, page 56
- Beef curry, page 88
- Pork and cider casserole, page 76
- Cheesy potato cakes, page 123
- Quick bifanas, page 75

STEAM ROASTED PORK & CRACKLING

This is one of the easiest roasts to cook on a Sunday for your dinner. We love how tender the pork is and how amazingly crispy and addictive the crackling is. We drizzle the rind with oil, then sprinkle with salt, as well as putting a delicious flavoursome garlic and mustard marinade on the meat. Serve this with our apple sauce on page 74.

....

SERVES **6**
FUNCTIONS **STEAM ROAST**
PREP **8 MINUTES**
STEAM ROAST COOK TIME **60 MINUTES**
TOTAL COOK TIME **60 MINUTES**
CALORIES **391**

....

- 1.1kg/2lb 7oz rolled and tied pork loin joint with skin
- 2 tsp mustard powder
- 1 tsp garlic powder
- 1 tsp mixed spice/apple spice
- 2 tbsp extra virgin olive oil
- 1 tsp rock salt
- 240ml/8½fl oz/1 cup vegetable or meat stock

01 An hour before you plan to roast your pork, prepare the crackling. Dab the skin dry with kitchen/paper towel, score the skin and place the pork uncovered on a plate in the fridge. After an hour, dab the skin again with the kitchen/paper towel and turn it over.

02 In a mixing bowl, combine the mustard powder, garlic powder, mixed spice and half the olive oil. Mix with a fork. Brush this over the bottom and sides of the pork, avoiding the skin.

03 Flip the pork back over and dab the skin one last time with the kitchen/paper towel to get rid of any last moisture. Rub the remaining olive oil all over the skin and give it a generous seasoning with the rock salt.

04 It's time to steam roast your pork. Add the stock to the bottom of the cooking pot, then set the air fryer basket/crisp plate in place. Add the pork, skin-side up.

05 Without a probe: press steam roast and set the temperature to 170°C/340°F and cook for 40 minutes. Increase the temperature to 180°C/360°F and cook for another 20 minutes, or until it reaches an internal temperature of 70°C/160°F or above.

06 With a probe: press the probe out of the machine (it's secured by a magnet). Remove the probe plug from in the lid and put it in a safe place. Connect the probe to the lid, pushing it in until it clicks. Insert the probe into the thickest part of the meat. Close the lid, being careful not to trap the probe wire. Press probe, then press the preset for pork. It will suggest 75°C/165°F. Select this and it will start cooking. It will stop once it reaches the suggested internal temperature. (We tested this with a timer/stop clock and found it took exactly an hour.)

07 When the multicooker beeps, remove the pork from the cooking pot, wrap it in foil, including the crackling, and leave to rest for 20 minutes before serving. We serve our pork with crackling and apple sauce (overleaf).

Finish with a Probe I like to add the probe after 40 minutes cooking at 170°C/340°F. That way as you can cook the pork at two temperatures, but still be sure to finish cooking when it reaches the right temperature.

Rinse & Repeat This method for cooking with a probe is the same system regardless of the meat or fish you are using. When cooking meats, such as lamb or beef, there are options for rare, medium rare and so on. Because the multicooker stops cooking when you reach the dream temperature, it means you don't have to worry about getting your lamb right; instead you can achieve perfect medium rare.

JAZZY APPLE SAUCE

SERVES **6**
FUNCTIONS **PRESSURE COOK**
PREP **10 MINUTES**
PRESSURE COOK TIME **6 MINUTES**
TOTAL COOK TIME **6 MINUTES**
CALORIES **185**

....

6 jazz apples
55g/2oz/¼ cup salted butter
4 heaped tbsp granulated sugar
2 tsp ground cinnamon
½ tsp mixed spice/apple spice

01 Add 240ml/8½fl oz/1 cup water to the cooking pot. Peel and chop the apples into small cubes, discarding the cores as you go. Add the apples to the water, spreading them out as you add them. Chop the butter into chunks and add it to the apples, then sprinkle 3 tablespoons of the sugar over the top.

02 Secure the pressure cooker lid, set the valve to sealing and pressure cook for 6 minutes, followed by a 3-minute natural pressure release.

03 After releasing pressure, drain the liquid from the apples and butter, then use a wooden spoon to break the apples up a bit. Sprinkle in the remaining sugar, the cinnamon and the mixed spice. Give it a stir and adjust the levels of sweetness and spice to taste.

CREAMY MUSHROOM SAUCE FOR EVERYTHING

SERVES **6**
FUNCTIONS **SAUTÉ**
PREP **10 MINUTES**
SAUTÉ COOK TIME **8 MINUTES**
TOTAL COOK TIME **8 MINUTES**
CALORIES **170**

....

1 tbsp extra virgin olive oil
1 medium brown onion
285g/10oz button mushrooms
2 sprigs of thyme
120ml/4fl oz/½ cup dry white wine
120ml/4fl oz/½ cup vegetable stock
1 × 150g/5½oz pack cream cheese (we use Boursin)
2 tsp dried thyme
1 tsp dried parsley
2 tsp garlic purée

01 Press the sauté button on your multicooker, add the olive oil and, as it warms up, peel and thinly slice the onion and half the mushrooms, if they are large. Add the onion to the cooking pot and wait for the sizzle. Sauté the onion and, once it has started to soften, add the mushrooms and fresh thyme. Sauté until the mushrooms are soft and the onion has started to get crispy.

02 Pour the white wine and stock into the pot and use a wooden spoon to scrape any bits stuck to the bottom.

03 Stir in the cream cheese, seasoning and garlic purée. Continue to stir until the sauce comes together, then cancel the sauté.

04 Season generously with salt and pepper, and leave the sauce to sit for a couple of minutes to thicken up before serving with your pork.

PORTUGUESE PORK KEBABS

SERVES **2**
FUNCTIONS **GRILL/BROIL**
PREP **5 MINUTES**
GRILL COOK TIME **10 MINUTES**
TOTAL COOK TIME **10 MINUTES**
CALORIES **721**

....

1 red (bell) pepper/capsicum
1 green (bell) pepper/capsicum
1 red onion
2 tsp smoked paprika
1 tsp piri piri dried seasoning
¼ tsp garlic powder
½ tsp ground coriander
1 tbsp extra virgin olive oil
1 tsp balsamic vinegar
6 chunky slices leftover roast pork (450g/1lb)

01 Slice and deseed the peppers and chop them into chunks. Peel and slice the onion into kebab-style wedges.

02 Place the dried seasonings in a small bowl with a generous seasoning of salt and pepper. Mix with a fork.

03 Place three-quarters of the seasoning in a medium bowl and add the peppers and onion. Pour in three-quarters of the olive oil and balsamic vinegar and mix well with your hands until everything is coated.

04 Add the air fryer basket/crisp plate to the cooking pot and spread out the seasoned vegetables. Press grill/broil and cook for 7 minutes at 240°C/465°F. Turn the vegetables halfway through.

05 Chop the pork into chunks and place in the medium bowl with the remaining dried seasoning, olive oil and vinegar. Mix with your hands until evenly coated. Place the pork and grilled vegetables onto 4 medium skewers, alternating between onion, different coloured peppers and the pork, until you have filled them all. Place the skewers into the air fryer basket/crisp plate and grill at the same temperature for 3 minutes.

06 Serve the kebabs with salad and flatbreads.

QUICK BIFANAS

SERVES **2**
FUNCTIONS **AIR FRY**
PREP **5 MINUTES**
AIR FRY COOK TIME **4 MINUTES**
TOTAL COOK TIME **4 MINUTES**
CALORIES **761**

....

1 garlic clove, minced
2 tsp extra virgin olive oil
1 tsp finely chopped fresh parsley
4 thin slices leftover roast pork (225g/8oz)
2 ciabatta rolls
Butter, for spreading
2 tsp mayonnaise (we use aioli)

01 Mix the garlic, olive oil and parsley in a little bowl. Brush the garlic mixture over the slices of pork, using a pastry brush.

02 Place the pork in the air fryer basket/crisp plate and air fry at 160°C/320°F for 4 minutes, or until heated through.

03 Meanwhile, butter the rolls and add 2 slices of the warmed pork to each one. Top with a spoonful of mayonnaise and serve.

LEFTOVER PORK CIDER CASSEROLE

My favourite part of a roast dinner is thinking about what I'm going to do with the leftover roasting meat! This creamy leftover pork casserole uses up spare veg, leftover pork, the apples the kids insisted I buy but didn't eat, and that can of cider I bought Dom ages ago that he didn't drink. It is leftover food heaven and it's easy to customise to fit different leftovers. This makes enough for two family dinners so you can put half in the freezer for another day.

SERVES **8**
FUNCTIONS **SAUTÉ, PRESSURE COOK**
PREP **12 MINUTES**
SAUTÉ COOK TIME **8 MINUTES**
PRESSURE COOK TIME **4 MINUTES**
TOTAL COOK TIME **12 MINUTES**
CALORIES **301**

1 large brown onion
3 small celery sticks
2 medium carrots
1 × 200g/7oz pack bacon lardons
Extra virgin olive oil
2 red apples (skin on)
1 leek
450g/1lb baby potatoes
480ml/17fl oz/2 cups vegetable or meat stock
480ml/17fl oz/2 cups sweet (hard) cider
1 tbsp apple sauce
1 tbsp wholegrain mustard
1 tbsp dried thyme
1 tsp garlic powder
1 heaped tbsp crème fraîche
225g/8oz roast pork (see page 73), chopped into 2cm/¾in chunks

01 Peel and thinly slice the onion, trim and chop the celery into 2cm/¾in chunks, and peel and chop the carrots into 2cm/¾in chunks. Add them to the cooking pot with the bacon bits and a drizzle of olive oil and press sauté. Wait for the sizzle, then sauté for about 5 minutes, or until the bacon is cooked.

02 Core and roughly chop the apples, and trim and finely chop the leek, then stir them into the pot. Cancel sauté. Halve the baby potatoes and add them to the pot. Pour in the stock and cider. Stir well, then secure the pressure cooker lid, set the valve to sealing and pressure cook for 4 minutes, followed by a quick pressure release.

03 After releasing the remaining pressure, add the apple sauce, wholegrain mustard, thyme, garlic powder and crème fraîche. The warmth of the pot will help create a creamy sauce. Use a stick blender to blend a small amount of the casserole, then stir. This will make it even thicker and more creamy.

04 Finally, add the cooked pork and set the multicooker to sauté for a couple of minutes, to warm the pork (or skip this step, if you plan to freeze the casserole).

05 Serve with mustard mash (see page 120).

Pork Casserole Mini Pies During the making of this book, we had spare pastry and knew we wouldn't be able to eat all the casserole, so we made mini pies with pastry hearts, just like you see in the marry me chicken pie on page 56. We used spare casserole for the filling and it was just as delicious. Steam bake them for 15 minutes at 180°C/360°F.

Freezer Casserole We filled two 18cm (7in) square foil trays to the top with this recipe. Each of those would easily feed us as a family of four. Because it isn't recommended to reheat meat twice, note that we only warm up the pork in step 04 if we're eating it straight away.

PORK & APPLE BURGERS WITH CHIPS

I love cooking burgers in the air fryer, but what makes them even better are the chips! These burgers are loaded with grated apple, apple sauce, red onion, thyme and mustard, and served with lightly spiced sweet potato chips.

SERVES **4**
FUNCTIONS **STEAM AIR FRY, AIR FRY**
PREP **12 MINUTES**
STEAM AIR FRY COOK TIME **20 MINUTES**
AIR FRY COOK TIME **18 MINUTES**
TOTAL COOK TIME **38 MINUTES**
CALORIES **899**

SWEET POTATO CHIPS
3 medium sweet potatoes
1 tbsp extra virgin olive oil
1 tsp dried basil
1 tsp mustard powder
½ tsp garlic powder

PORK APPLE BURGERS
1 red apple
½ medium red onion
500g/1lb 2oz minced/ground pork
1 heaped tbsp apple sauce
½ tsp Dijon mustard
1 tsp fresh thyme leaves
1 tsp mixed herbs/Italian seasoning
28g/1oz/½ cup panko breadcrumbs

BURGER SAUCE
3 heaped tbsp mayonnaise
2 tsp apple sauce
2 tsp finely chopped chives
½ tsp mustard powder
½ tsp garlic powder
1 tsp dried thyme

BURGER GARNISH
Handful Little Gem lettuce leaves
2 medium tomatoes
4 brioche buns

01 Start by making the sweet potato chips. Peel and chop the sweet potatoes into chunky chips. Place them in a mixing bowl with the olive oil and seasonings. Mix well with your hands until the chips are thoroughly coated. Tip them into the air fryer basket/crisp plate inside the cooking pot and spread them out. Press steam air fry and cook at 180°C/360°F for 20 minutes.

02 Remove the sweet potatoes from the air fryer basket and set aside.

03 Chop the red apple into chunks and discard the core. Keep the skin on as it adds a lovely texture and colour to your burgers. Peel the onion and cut it in half. Place the apple and onion in a food processor or blender and blitz until finely chopped. Tip them into a mixing bowl and add the pork and the remaining burger ingredients. Mix well with your hands. Use a burger press or your hands to turn the mixture into 4 equal-sized burgers.

04 Place the air fryer basket/crisp plate in the multicooker and add the burgers in an even layer. You may have to cook them in batches, depending on the size of your multicooker. Set the temperature to 180°C/360°F and air fry for 15 minutes.

05 In the meantime, place all the burger sauce ingredients in a small bowl, reserving some of the chives, and mix well. Get your salad garnish ingredients ready – shred the lettuce and slice the tomatoes.

06 When the multicooker beeps, remove the burgers and place the sweet potato chips in the air fryer basket/crisp plate to finish them off. If you like crispy sweet potato chips, opt for 200°C/400°F, otherwise opt for 180°C/360°F. Either way, cook the chips for a final 3 minutes.

07 Whilst they are warming up, spread the sauce on the tops and bottoms of the brioche buns, then add some lettuce, tomato, a burger patty, lots more burger sauce and a sprinkling of the reserved chives. When the multicooker beeps, add the chips to your dinner plates and tuck in.

MUST TRY DIET COLA GAMMON

This is one of the greatest things to do with gammon and is perfect for getting rid of the salty taste without needing to soak the gammon first. If you live in the US, gammon is what us Brits call ham before it has been cooked.

....

SERVES **8**
FUNCTIONS **SAUTÉ, PRESSURE COOK**
PREP **5 MINUTES**
SAUTÉ COOK TIME **5 MINUTES**
PRESSURE COOK TIME **40 MINUTES**
TOTAL COOK TIME **45 MINUTES**
CALORIES **234**

....

1 medium brown onion
1 tbsp extra virgin olive oil
2 tsp frozen chopped garlic
240ml/8½fl oz/1 cup vegetable stock
1.2kg/2½lb boneless gammon joint/ham, skinless but with a good layer of fat
1.25l/42fl oz/5 cups diet cola

01 Peel and dice the onion. Press sauté on the pressure cooker, add the olive oil and onion and wait for the sizzle. Sauté until the onion has softened.

02 Cancel sauté and stir in the frozen garlic. Deglaze the cooking pot with the stock.

03 Place the gammon in the cooking pot and pour over the cola. Make sure you are pouring the cola over the gammon and not down the sides of it. You want the cola to soak into the gammon, which will reduce the salty taste.

04 Secure the pressure cooker lid, set the valve to sealing and pressure cook for 40 minutes, followed by a quick pressure release.

05 Remove the lid and use a fork to quickly remove the gammon, shaking off the excess liquid as you do this. Wrap the gammon tightly in foil and leave to rest for about 20 minutes, before slicing and serving.

Swap the Drink This method works with lots of different drinks. Whilst cola is our firm favourite, you can swap it for whatever you have in.

Swap the Drink to Fanta Swap the onion for a quartered orange and pour over Fanta. It tastes lovely and sweet.

Swap the Drink to Cider Swap the onion for 2 apples (chopped up with the skin left on) and pour over 4 × 440ml/16fl oz cans of sweet (hard) cider.

Don't Want to Add Shop-bought Drinks? Swap the cans for 960ml/34fl oz/4 cups water. And avoid shop-bought stock, as this can be salty and so can gammon.

Prefer to Slow Cook Your Gammon? Press slow cook on the multicooker and adjust to high. Slow cook for 4 hours, or until the gammon reaches an internal temperature of 70°C/160°F or above.

Pulled Gammon Turn the gammon into a pulled version, by increasing the slow cook time to 6 hours on high – it'll just fall apart – then smoother it in barbecue sauce.

LANCASHIRE HOTPOT WITH A TWIST

I love a hotpot, especially when I'm making it with kitchen gadgets. This casserole is slow cooked and the potato topping is air fried. The best of both worlds. We've put a Spanish twist on the Lancashire classic by swapping bacon for chorizo.

....

SERVES **4**
FUNCTIONS **SAUTÉ, SLOW COOK, AIR FRY, STEAM**
PREP **10 MINUTES**
SAUTÉ COOK TIME **5 MINUTES**
SLOW COOK TIME **3 HOURS**
AIR FRY COOK TIME **20 MINUTES**
STEAM COOK TIME **0 MINUTES**
TOTAL COOK TIME **3 HOURS 25 MINUTES**
CALORIES **887**

....

1 medium brown onion
2 tbsp salted butter
675g/1½lb lamb shoulder, boneless
130g/4½oz chorizo
240ml/8½fl oz/1 cup red wine
240ml/8½fl oz/1 cup lamb or beef stock
250g/9oz/1 cup passata
3 medium carrots
1 tbsp dried thyme
1 tbsp roughly chopped fresh curly parsley
1 tbsp Worcestershire sauce
1 tbsp tomato purée/paste
160g/5½oz/1 cup each frozen sweetcorn and garden peas

POTATO TOPPING
2 medium white potatoes
1 tbsp extra virgin olive oil
5 sprigs of thyme, leaves picked

01 Peel and finely chop the onion. Press sauté, add the onion and butter to the cooking pot and wait for the sizzle. Sauté the onions until softened.

02 Dice the lamb and add to the cooking pot until browned on all sides. Chop the chorizo, then add it to the pot, giving it a quick sauté, as you don't want it too crispy.

03 Cancel sauté and pour in the red wine, stock and passata, and deglaze the cooking pot with a wooden spoon.

04 Peel and cut the carrots into 1cm/½in half-moons, then add them to the pot with the thyme, parsley, Worcestershire sauce and tomato purée, along with a generous seasoning of salt and pepper. Give it a really good stir. Secure the lid and set it to slow cook for 3 hours.

05 When there is just 5 minutes left, prepare the potato topping. Scrub and thinly slice the potatoes and discard the ends. Place them in a mixing bowl with the olive oil and thyme and season with salt and pepper. Mix together with your hands to get an even coating.

06 Stir the casserole in the pot (you will instantly feel hungry from the smell of the lamb!) and decorate the top with the sliced potatoes, overlapping them to create a hotpot.

07 Place the air fryer lid on and air fry at 180°C/360°F for 20 minutes.

08 Whilst you are portioning up dinner, add 240ml/8½fl oz/1 cup water to the cooking pot and scrape down the bottom and sides. Add the frozen peas and sweetcorn to a multicooker-safe container and steam them for 0 minutes. This will help clean your cooking pot and will also warm your peas and corn. Serve the veg alongside the hotpot and season with salt and pepper.

SHEPHERD'S PIE WITH MEATY MASH

This is my favourite way to make a shepherd's pie – and the best bit is the way we cook the mash – the potatoes are stacked over the lamb, so juices bubble up to create the most flavoursome and colourful mash.

SERVES **6**
FUNCTIONS **SAUTÉ, PRESSURE COOK, AIR FRY**
PREP **12 MINUTES**
SAUTÉ COOK TIME **8 MINUTES**
PRESSURE COOK TIME **8 MINUTES**
AIR FRY COOK TIME **8 MINUTES**
TOTAL COOK TIME **24 MINUTES**
CALORIES **746**

1 medium brown onion
2 tsp salted butter
750g/1lb 10oz minced/ground lamb
240ml/8½fl oz/1 cup red wine
240ml/8½fl oz/1 cup vegetable stock
500g/1lb 2oz/2 cups passata
2 celery sticks
2 medium carrots
1 tbsp dried thyme
1 tbsp dried parsley
1 tbsp Worcestershire sauce
1 tbsp tomato purée/paste
2 tbsp lamb gravy granules
320g/11½oz/2 cups frozen garden peas

FLAVOURED MASH
1.8kg/4lb white potatoes
1½ tbsp salted butter
2 tbsp whole/full-fat milk
2 tsp mixed herbs/Italian seasoning
1 tbsp roughly chopped fresh parsley
1 tbsp grated Parmesan

01 Peel and finely chop the onion. Press sauté, then add the onion to the cooking pot with the butter and wait for the sizzle. Sauté until the onion has softened. Add the lamb and stir with a wooden spoon to brown on all sides (don't cook the meat fully, as the pressure cooker will do this).

02 Cancel sauté and pour in the red wine, stock and passata, and deglaze the cooking pot.

03 Trim and finely chop the celery, peel and finely chop the carrots, then add them to the pot with the thyme, parsley, Worcestershire sauce and tomato purée. Give it a really good stir.

04 Place the steamer basket over the lamb filling. (Don't use a tall trivet because you want the lamb juices to bubble up and flavour the potatoes.) Peel and quarter the potatoes for the flavoured mash, place them in the steamer basket and season them with salt and pepper. Secure the pressure cooker lid, set the valve to sealing and pressure cook for 8 minutes, followed by a quick pressure release.

05 Carefully remove the steamer basket and transfer the potatoes to a mixing bowl. The potatoes will be slightly orange from the lamb juices (looking like sweet potatoes) and the flavour will be incredible. Add the butter, milk, mixed herbs and fresh parsley to the potatoes, as well as some salt and pepper, and use a fork to mash them to a smooth consistency.

06 Meanwhile, press sauté on the multicooker, stir the filling, and add the gravy granules, along with the frozen peas. Allow it to bubble up to reduce the liquid a little. Generously season to taste with salt and pepper, and adjust with extra thyme, if needed. Press cancel.

07 Top the lamb with the mashed potatoes, then sprinkle with the Parmesan. Place the air fryer lid on the multicooker and air fry at 200°C/400°F for 8 minutes, to create an incredible crust on the mash.

Lazy Mash The brilliance of using the multicooker for mashed potatoes is that they become so tender you can mash them quickly with a fork without needing to put in the effort of a potato masher.

IRISH BEEF STEW & DUMPLINGS

The first thing I ever cooked in a kitchen gadget was a beef stew and dumplings. It was a disaster, as the slow cooker my mum had given me was broken (she didn't know it!). But it made me want to buy my own slow cooker and, fast forward more than 20 years, I always make several beef stews in the slow cooker over winter months.

SERVES **6**
FUNCTIONS **SAUTÉ, SLOW COOK, AIR FRY**
PREP **12 MINUTES**
SAUTÉ COOK TIME **8 MINUTES**
SLOW COOK TIME **3 HOURS**
AIR FRY COOK TIME **10 MINUTES**
TOTAL COOK TIME **3 HOURS 18 MINUTES**
CALORIES **743**

2 × 440ml/16fl oz cans stout (we use Guinness)
675g/1½lb diced beef (we use shin)
2 tbsp salted butter
1 medium brown onion
2 celery sticks
4 medium carrots
3 medium white potatoes
1 tbsp tomato purée/paste
1 tbsp dried rosemary
1 tbsp dried thyme
4 heaped tbsp beef gravy granules
160g/5¾oz/1 cup frozen garden peas
1 tbsp roughly chopped fresh thyme

SUET DUMPLINGS
100g/3½oz shredded suet
200g/7oz/1½ cups self-raising/self-rising flour
2 tsp dried rosemary
2 tsp mixed herbs/Italian seasoning

01 An hour before you plan to start, open the cans of stout and let them sit so they are flat and not frothy.

02 Press sauté, add the diced beef, along with the butter, and brown on all sides. Peel and thinly slice the onion, trim and thinly sliced the celery, peel and chop the carrots into 1cm/½in chunks and peel and chop the potatoes into 2cm/¾in chunks. Add them to the pot with the beef and stir to coat everything in the butter, then press cancel.

03 Deglaze the pot with the stout, pouring it all in (it is a replacement for stock).

04 Add the tomato purée, rosemary and thyme and stir. Secure the lid on the multicooker (you may need to add the pressure cooker lid) and press slow cook for 3 hours on high or 5½ hours on low.

05 In the meantime, make your suet dumplings. Place the suet and flour in a mixing bowl, along with the seasonings. Pour in 80ml/2¾fl oz/⅓ cup water, a little at a time, mixing until you have a dough. Flour your hands, then dust the dough with flour and stretch and fold until you have a smooth dough. Divide the dough into either 6 large, 8 medium, or 12 small dumplings, depending on how you like them.

06 When the slow cooker has finished its 3 or 5½ hours, give it a good stir and, as you are stirring, add the gravy granules, frozen peas, fresh thyme and some salt and pepper. Place the dumplings on top of the stew, spreading them out evenly as you do. Add the lid back on and air fry for 10 minutes at 180°C/360°F or until you have beautiful golden dumplings.

No Suet If you don't like suet or can't source it, then swap the dumpling recipe here for our cheesy dumplings on page 136 and keep the same time and temp.

Mini Meat Pies If you have leftovers, my favourite thing to make is mini pies. Load ramekins or small pie dishes to the brim with leftover beef stew, then cover with puff pastry. Make a slit in the top of the pastry with a knife, then brush with egg wash and they are ready to air fry. You can freeze them before the egg wash for another day. Just defrost when you want to cook them. Place the pies on the air fryer basket/crisp plate in the cooking pot and air fry at 180°C/360°F for 20–25 minutes, depending on the size of the pie.

What is the Best Cut of Beef for a Stew? We love using beef shin. We get it when it's available and freeze it for later. You can use any slow-cooking beef cut, though, and other favourites include beef cheeks or braising/chuck steak.

LEFTOVER BEEF MASSAMAN CURRY

Whilst on holiday a few years ago, I ate the most amazing massaman curry. It is a creamy Thai curry loaded with beef and potatoes. Back home, I wanted to recreate it, so I have done just that using dehydrated roast beef leftovers (see page 34). You could make it vegetarian by swapping the beef for a can of drained chickpeas and using veg stock.

．．．．．．．．．．．．．．．．．．．．．．．．．．．．．．．．．．．．．

SERVES **6**
FUNCTIONS **SAUTÉ, PRESSURE COOK**
PREP **6 MINUTES**
SAUTÉ COOK TIME **5 MINUTES**
PRESSURE COOK TIME **4 MINUTES**
TOTAL COOK TIME **9 MINUTES**
CALORIES **427**

．．．．．．．．．．．．．．．．．．．．．．．．．．．．．．．．．．．．．

1 medium red onion
1 tbsp extra virgin olive oil
750g/1lb 10oz white potatoes
225g/8oz leftover roast beef
1 tsp lemongrass paste
1 tsp ginger purée
1 tsp garlic purée
2 tbsp massaman curry paste
2 tsp ground coriander
2 tsp ground cumin
Lime wedges, to serve
Roughly chopped coriander/cilantro, to serve

CURRY SAUCE
1 tbsp massaman curry paste
240ml/8½fl oz/1 cup beef stock
2 tsp lemongrass paste
2 tsp tomato purée/paste
1 tbsp ginger purée
500g/1lb 2oz/2 cups passata
1 x 400g/14oz can coconut milk (not coconut cream)

01 Peel and finely chop the onion. Press sauté, then add the onion to the cooking pot with the olive oil and wait for the sizzle. Continue cooking until the onion has softened. Press cancel, add in all the curry sauce ingredients and give it a good stir.

02 Peel and chop the potatoes into 2cm/¾in chunks, add them to the pot and stir again. Secure the pressure cooker lid, set the valve to sealing and pressure cook for 4 minutes, followed by a quick pressure release.

03 After releasing the pressure, give it a stir. Chop the leftover roast beef into 2cm/¾in chunks and add it to the pot with all the remaining ingredients. Stir and use the heat from the pressure cooking to warm the beef through. (If the cooking pot has gone cold, you can press sauté to heat through for a couple of minutes.)

04 Serve with coconut jasmine rice from page 166, a lime wedge and some chopped coriander.

Freezer Friendly This curry is delicious made ahead, frozen and reheated another day. Cook up to the point of adding the beef, then instead of heating the beef through, stir it into the ingredients and transfer to freezer containers.

ROSEMARY & THYME SCOTCH EGGS

Hard-boiled eggs are a bucket list recipe for making with the pressure cook button or the air fryer button. When I persuade other people to try it, they don't stop talking about it for months, because they are that good. If I was to share just one recipe using hard-boiled eggs, it would be these delicious scotch eggs. You pressure cook the eggs, add yummy rosemary-and-thyme-flavoured sausage meat, then create a bowl system for the flour, egg and breadcrumbs, and finally air fry to perfection.

SERVES **6**
FUNCTIONS **PRESSURE COOK, AIR FRY**
PREP **10 MINUTES**
PRESSURE COOK TIME **6 MINUTES**
AIR FRY COOK TIME **20 MINUTES**
TOTAL COOK TIME **26 MINUTES**
CALORIES **570**

6 large eggs
70g/2½oz/½ cup plain/all-purpose flour
1 large egg
115g/4oz/¾ cup golden breadcrumbs (we use Paxo)

SAUSAGE MEAT LAYER
675g/1½lb Cumberland sausages
2 tbsp dried thyme
2 tbsp dried rosemary
2 tbsp smoked paprika
2 tsp garlic powder

GARDEN SALAD
Handful Little Gem lettuce leaves
¼ cucumber
6 cherry tomatoes

01 Place 240ml/8½fl oz/1 cup water in your cooking pot. Add a steamer basket, then carefully add your eggs to prevent them cracking. Secure the pressure cooker lid, set the valve to sealing and pressure cook the eggs for 6 minutes, followed by a quick pressure release. Alternatively, place the eggs in the air fryer basket/crisp plate and air fry or bake for 14 minutes at 120°C/250°F.

02 Meanwhile, prepare the sausage meat. Using a clean chopping board, cut a slit down the side of the sausages; this will make it easy to peel the skin off. Remove the skin and place the sausage meat in a bowl with all the seasonings. Mix everything well with your hands for a few minutes, to make sure the seasoning is distributed throughout the meat.

03 Place the flour in a shallow bowl, crack the egg into another and add the breadcrumbs to a third bowl. Beat the egg with a fork.

04 After releasing the pressure on the multicooker, peel the eggs under a cold tap. Add a layer of sausage meat around each of the eggs. (We find the best way to do this is to weigh the sausage meat and divide it by 6, to make sure each egg is equally covered.)

05 One at a time, carefully roll the scotch eggs in the flour, then drench them in the egg, then roll them in the breadcrumbs, making sure they get a good coating of each.

06 Carefully place them in the air fryer basket/crisp plate inside the cooking pot. Air fry at 180°C/360°F for 20 minutes. Don't turn them over during cooking, as they are too delicate.

07 We love scotch eggs over salad. Add Little Gem lettuce leaves to a picnic box, then toss in some chunky quartered cucumber and halved cherry tomatoes.

Chef Dom Tip Use one hand for the flour and egg, and the other for the breadcrumbs. It will save constantly washing your hands.

The Ultimate Boiled Eggs So, you're probably wondering what the big deal is with kitchen gadget eggs? After all, everyone does it and, once you have one, you don't go back to boiling them in a pan. Well, firstly, it's an act of science with the time and temperature, so you don't have to worry that you've boiled them for too long or not long enough. But mostly, because boiled eggs in the air fryer or the pressure cooker peel so easily. Simply rinse them under a cold water tap as you peel them, and they are perfect every single time. You can use them for scotch eggs, for egg mayo (see page 118), for devilled eggs, a tuna salad, or however you like to serve them.

If You Love Boiled Eggs For soft boiled, choose 2 minutes pressure cooking or 10–12 minutes air frying, and for hard boiled try 16-18 minutes.

ULTIMATE STEAK SHARING TRAY

At our favourite steak restaurant, they do a sharing board. It's not cheap, so we thought we'd do our own version as a fantastic end to our meat chapter.

....

SERVES **2**
FUNCTIONS **AIR FRY, GRILL/BROIL**
PREP **20 MINUTES**
AIR FRY COOK TIME **19 MINUTES**
GRILL/BROIL COOK TIME **19 MINUTES**
TOTAL COOK TIME **38 MINUTES**
CALORIES **1651**

....

1 × 225g/8oz ribeye steak
1 × 225g/8oz sirloin/porterhouse steak
4 tbsp mayonnaise
1 tbsp finely chopped fresh basil
12 black peppercorns
¼ tsp ground black pepper (to taste)
1 × portion chips (see page 113)
1 × portion Texas toast (see page 201)
¼ yellow or green courgette/zucchini
¼ aubergine/eggplant
½ red (bell) pepper/capsicum
170g/6oz cherry tomatoes, halved
85g/3oz button mushrooms, halved
1 tbsp extra virgin olive oil
1 tsp dried basil

STEAK MARINADE
2 tbsp balsamic vinegar
1 tbsp Worcestershire sauce
1 tbsp soy sauce
1 tbsp extra virgin olive oil
¼ tsp garlic powder
1 tbsp finely chopped fresh basil
1 tsp Dijon mustard

CHORIZO PEAS
55g/2oz chorizo
80g/3oz/½ cup frozen garden peas
55g/2oz/¼ cup salted butter
55g/2oz/½ cup grated Gouda cheese

01 Place the steak marinade ingredients in a bowl and mix well. Separate the marinade equally between 2 shallow bowls. Place the steaks in one of the bowls and flip them over to give them a good coating. Place in the fridge for later.

02 Make your two mayonnaises now, as they can be stored in the fridge for later. Place 2 heaped tablespoons of mayonnaise in one sauce dish, and 2 heaped tablespoons in another. Add 2 teaspoons of the reserved steak marinade to one bowl, along with a tablespoon of the finely chopped basil and mix well. Add the peppercorns and ground pepper to your preferred taste to the second bowl of mayonnaise. Place in the fridge until needed.

03 Next, cook the chorizo peas. Slice the chorizo and add it to the cooking pot. Air fry for 5 minutes at 180°C/360°F. Tip the cooked chorizo into a small serving dish, along with the frozen peas and butter. Place the dish in the air fryer basket/crisp plate inside the cooking pot and air fry for another 5 minutes at 180°C/360°F, or until the butter has melted and the peas are warmed through. Sprinkle the grated cheese over the chorizo peas and set aside (the cheese will melt as the peas warm it up).

04 Prepare the chips (see page 113) but reduce the cooking time by 3 minutes to finish them later. Cook the Texas toast (see page 201) and set aside.

05 Now, let's grill the veg. Chop the courgette and aubergine into 2cm/¾in slices, then halve them. Deseed and quarter the pepper. Add all the prepared veg to a mixing bowl along with the olive oil, dried basil and a generous seasoning of salt and pepper. Mix well with your hands. Leave the cherry tomatoes and mushrooms in the bowl, as they are quick cooking, but place everything else in the air fryer basket/crisp plate, spreading it out. Press grill/broil and cook at 240°C/465°F for 8 minutes. Give the vegetables a shake, add the cherry tomatoes and mushrooms, and cook for a further 5 minutes at the same temperature.

06 Place the veg on a serving platter and add the steaks to the air fryer basket/crisp plate. Press grill and cook at 240°C/465°F for 3 minutes, flip over and do the same again on the other side. Remove the steaks and set aside to rest. Finally, slice them into 1cm/½in strips and add to the sharing tray.

07 Now that you have done the steak and grilled veg, you can finish the other ingredients. Start by adding the chips to the air fryer basket/crisp plate in the cooking pot. Spread them out then air fry for 3 minutes at 160°C/320°F. Place the chips on the platter. Place the Texas toast and chorizo peas in the air fryer basket/crisp plate and cook them for the same time at the same temperature to warm. Add everything to the platter, place the little pots of mayonnaise alongside and finish with a drizzle of the reserved marinade. It's now ready for serving.

HOW TO STEAM FISH

The first thing we ever steamed was fish fillets. More specifically, hake fillets. They were gorgeous, flaky and white and were cooked perfectly, but they were bland and boring. To kickstart our fish chapter, we wanted to share with you tips on how to cook fish fillets using the steam function, in order to show how incredibly fast they cook and, best of all, to show how to season them quickly to perfection.

STEAMED FISH & STEAMED SIDES COOKING TIMES

- **Basa Fillets** and 2cm/¾in butternut squash cubes (both 6 minutes)
- **Salmon Fillets** (6 minutes) and frozen broccoli (3 minutes) or pasta bows (10 minutes)
- **Cod Fillets** (7 minutes) and trimmed green beans (8 minutes) or quinoa (6 minutes)
- **Haddock Fillets** (8 minutes) and sliced mushrooms (4 minutes)
- **Seabass Fillets** (5 minutes) and jasmine rice (10 minutes)

5-MINUTE SPICED SEABASS

Seabass fillets are brilliant because they are thinner than salmon and cod fillets, so they cook more quickly. I sprinkle them with some shawarma seasoning for a burst of flavour.

SERVES **2**
FUNCTIONS **STEAM**
PREP **3 MINUTES**
STEAM COOK TIME **5 MINUTES**
TOTAL COOK TIME **5 MINUTES**
CALORIES **279**

2 tbsp extra virgin olive oil
1 tbsp shawarma seasoning
¼ tsp garlic powder
2 seabass fillets, skin on
Squeeze of lemon

01 Add the olive oil, shawarma seasoning and garlic powder to a small bowl. Mix well with a fork.

02 Place the seabass fillets skin-side down on a chopping board and season generously with salt and pepper. Using a pastry brush, coat the tops of the fillets with the shawarma paste to form a crust (the oil in the paste will help it stick).

03 Place 240ml/8½fl oz/1 cup liquid in the cooking pot (you could use water, stock, or a combination of these), then add the air fryer basket/crisp plate. Place the fish on top, then secure the multicooker lid and steam for 5 minutes.

04 When the multicooker beeps, you will have steamed seabass. And, yes, it's not a typo – it really only takes 5 minutes! Serve with a squeeze of lemon.

STEAMED FISH 101

Raid Your Herbs & Spices Drawer You can easily replace the shawarma seasoning for another favourite seasoning mix. I love my shop-bought coconut lime and Caribbean curry powder. You could try a Cajun or taco seasoning, or keep it simple with some mixed herbs. Just remember, use ½ tablespoon of dried seasoning per fish fillet.

Any Fish Fillet You can mix and match this recipe with any favourite fish fillet – skin on or skin off. We love cod, haddock, basa, pollock and, of course, salmon.

Season But No Crust If you would rather have the fish with seasoning but without the crust, this is easy to do, too. Simply leave out the oil and sprinkle the seasoning directly on to the fish.

Fish & Veg Now, who just eats fish on its own? It's always a meal, right? So, you can steam the fish and vegetables together – and season the veg at the same time. If the vegetables take slightly longer to cook than the fish, then start them off first. Just add the fish when the remaining veg cooking time is just 5 minutes and they can be ready together.

Fish & Grains Just like with fish and veg, you can cook your fish and grains together. Just add quinoa, jasmine rice or another favourite to the cooking pot, then place the fish on the air fryer rack in the top position or on the crisp plate on top. For cooking times, see opposite.

BROCCOLI-CRUSTED SALMON

My favourite lunchtime trio is salmon, broccoli and potatoes. Dom and I often have this when the kids are at school. Here I have taken those three main ingredients and transformed them into a delicious lunch for two. Broccoli is mixed with garlic and basil to make a delicious crust for the salmon and it is served alongside perfectly crispy baby potatoes and the remaining broccoli.

SERVES **2**
FUNCTIONS **STEAM ROAST, STEAM**
PREP **12 MINUTES**
STEAM ROAST COOK TIME **15 MINUTES**
STEAM COOK TIME **2 MINUTES**
TOTAL COOK TIME **17 MINUTES**
CALORIES **757**

1 × 30g/1oz bag fresh basil
2 × 115g/4oz salmon fillets

BABY POTATOES
225g/8oz baby potatoes
1 tbsp extra virgin olive oil
1 tbsp lemon juice
1 tbsp mixed herbs/Italian seasoning

BROCCOLI CRUST
170g/6oz small broccoli florets
1 tbsp dried dill
150g/5½oz crème fraîche
1 tbsp lemon juice
1 tbsp garlic purée

01 Place the baby potatoes in a bowl. If any of them are particularly large, cut them in half to make them all an equal size. Add the olive oil, lemon juice and mixed herbs to the bowl. Roughly chop half the basil leaves and add them, too. Mix everything together with your hands to get an even coating.

02 Pour 360ml/12½fl oz/1½ cups water into the cooking pot and add the air fryer basket/crisp plate. Tip in the potatoes and set to steam roast at 180°C/360°F for 9 minutes.

03 Meanwhile, place half the broccoli florets in a food processor or blender with the remaining basil leaves and the dried dill. Blitz until it resembles coarse breadcrumbs. Transfer to a shallow bowl.

04 In another shallow bowl, combine the crème fraîche, lemon juice and garlic purée, and mix well. Transfer a quarter of this mixture into a small bowl to serve alongside the salmon and potatoes.

05 Create a foil packet for the salmon by folding 2 sheets of foil the size of your cooking pot over each other in the shape of a cross. Bring the sides up to create a boat. Coat the salmon fillets in the remaining crème fraîche mixture, then cover them in the broccoli crumb. Place them in the foil packets.

06 When the multicooker beeps, check the baby potatoes are fork tender and there is enough water to go back to steam, then place the foil packets of salmon on top of the potatoes. Steam roast them both together for 6 minutes at the same temperature.

07 Remove the salmon and place on your dinner plates. Add the remaining broccoli florets to the cooking pot and steam for 2 minutes or until the broccoli is fork tender.

08 Serve the salmon with the potatoes and broccoli, giving them a generous seasoning of salt and pepper, with the reserved sauce on the side.

PRAWN & HALLOUMI ORZOTTO

Orzotto is a fun recipe to make when you can't decide between pasta or rice for dinner. Orzo is pasta that bears a striking resemblance to risotto rice, and is cooked with the ingredients that typically go into a risotto. In this orzotto recipe, we use prawns and halloumi for a real summer treat.

....

SERVES **4**
FUNCTIONS **SAUTÉ, PRESSURE COOK, AIR FRY**
PREP **5 MINUTES**
SAUTÉ COOK TIME **4 MINUTES**
PRESSURE COOK TIME **3 MINUTES**
AIR FRY COOK TIME **15 MINUTES**
TOTAL COOK TIME **22 MINUTES**
CALORIES **634**

....

1 medium red onion
55g/2oz/¼ cup salted butter (straight from the fridge)
240ml/8½fl oz/1 cup dry white wine
1 tbsp frozen chopped garlic
360ml/12½fl oz/1½ cups vegetable stock
175g/6oz/1 cup orzo pasta
1 tbsp finely chopped fresh oregano
1 tbsp dried basil
2 tbsp balsamic vinegar
4 tbsp crème fraîche
115g/4oz halloumi cheese
250g/9oz frozen raw peeled super king prawns/shrimp
2 tsp roughly chopped fresh basil
Lemon, for squeezing
Rocket/arugula, to serve

01 Peel and thinly slice the red onion, then add it to the cooking pot along with the butter, chopping it into chunks as you add it. (It's better to use fridge-temperature butter as otherwise it melts too quickly and will burn in the cooking pot.) Press sauté and wait for the sizzle, then sauté the onion until softened.

02 Cancel sauté and deglaze the cooking pot with the white wine. Stir in the frozen garlic and pour in the stock. Add the pasta and mix well. Make sure all the orzo grains are below the level of the liquid.

03 Secure the lid and pressure cook for 3 minutes, followed by a 10-minute natural pressure release.

04 After releasing the remaining pressure, add the oregano and dried basil, the balsamic vinegar and the crème fraîche, and give it a good stir.

05 Cut the halloumi into 2cm/¾in chunks, then add them to the cooking pot with the frozen prawns. Secure the lid and air fry at 180°C/360°F for 15 minutes.

06 Serve with a sprinkling of fresh basil, rocket leaves and a squeeze of lemon.

20-MINUTE LEMON PEPPER FISH GOUJONS

I went to a cooking class last year and learnt how to fillet plaice. It was a great skill to learn, but when I looked at the flat fish, it made me realise just how much waste there is. In the class we sliced the plaice and made it into goujons. I took them home and, of course, air fried them, but it made me want to make goujons again, without the long filleting process. These lemon pepper fish goujons take just 20 minutes, including the prep time. We have swapped plaice for basa, as it's a brilliant fish for breading and is budget-friendly, too.

....

SERVES **4**
FUNCTIONS **AIR FRY**
PREP **8 MINUTES**
AIR FRY COOK TIME **12 MINUTES**
TOTAL COOK TIME **12 MINUTES**
CALORIES **339**

....

2 × 240g/8½oz packs basa fillets
Juice of 3 lemons
70g/2½oz/½ cup plain/all-purpose flour
2 large eggs, beaten
75g/3oz/⅔ cup golden breadcrumbs (we use Paxo)
Lemon wedges, to serve

LEMON PEPPER RUB
½ tsp garlic powder
2 tbsp dried dill
1 tsp sea salt
1½ tsp ground black pepper
Zest of 3 lemons

LEMON MAYONNAISE
4 heaped tbsp mayonnaise
2 tsp dried dill

01 Firstly, place the lemon pepper rub ingredients in a bowl and mix well. When grating the lemon, we find a zester works best. Avoid the white part of the lemon, as it's very bitter.

02 Using a clean chopping board, cut the fish into goujons. Transfer them to a shallow bowl. Cover the fillets in the lemon juice – saving 2 teaspoons for the lemon mayonnaise – then tip in the rub ingredients and give it a good shake, so all the fish is coated evenly (you don't want one very peppery goujon!).

03 Set up your breading production line, as we like to call it – place the flour in one shallow bowl, the beaten eggs in another and the breadcrumbs in a final bowl.

04 Doing a few goujons at a time, coat them in the flour, then drench with the egg and finally dip into the breadcrumbs, making sure it all gets a good coating.

05 Pop the air fryer basket/crisp plate into the cooking pot and add the goujons. They need to be cooked in a single layer, so you may need to do this in batches. Set it to air fry at 180°C/360°F for 12 minutes.

06 Meanwhile, place the lemon mayonnaise ingredients with the reserved 2 teaspoons of lemon juice in a serving bowl and mix well.

07 When the crispy goujons are done, serve with lemon wedges and the lemon mayonnaise alongside.

PRAWN CURRY IN A HURRY

When we talk about using a multicooker, we talk a lot about the pressure cooker, air fryer and slow cooker functions, but there is never enough love for the sauté and how it is like cooking on the stove with a pan. In this recipe, we make a quick curry with the sauté function, then, by using the air fryer to reduce the sauce, we cook the naan bread at the same time.

SERVES **2**
FUNCTIONS **SAUTÉ, AIR FRY**
PREP **8 MINUTES**
SAUTÉ COOK TIME **7 MINUTES**
AIR FRY COOK TIME **4 MINUTES**
TOTAL COOK TIME **11 MINUTES**
CALORIES **531**

400g/14oz frozen raw peeled king prawns/shrimp
2 tsp extra virgin olive oil
2 tsp garam masala
1 tsp ground coriander
½ tsp garlic purée
½ tsp ginger purée
1 × 450g/1lb jar curry sauce (we use jalfrezi)
2 mini frozen naan breads
1 tbsp finely chopped fresh coriander/cilantro

01 Add the frozen prawns and the olive oil to your cooking pot and press sauté. When you start to hear the sizzle, it's time to sauté your prawns. I love watching prawns changing colour into that beautiful pink. When half of the prawns have changed colour, add the seasonings. Stir in the garam masala, coriander, garlic and ginger purées, and a generous amount of salt and pepper.

02 Keep sautéing and, when all the prawns are pink, stir in the curry sauce and cancel sauté.

03 Add the rack/crisp plate or a trivet in the top position over the curry, then place the naan breads on top (make sure they are above the curry and not in it). Secure the air fryer lid and air fry at 180°C/360°F for 4 minutes. (Air frying the naan like this also does a great job of reducing the sauce and acts like a simmer.)

04 When the air fryer beeps, sprinkle fresh coriander over the curry and serve it with the naan bread alongside.

Pepper & Onion Prefer more texture to your curry? Start by sautéing with 1 tablespoon of olive oil instead of 2 teaspoons and add 1 finely chopped red (bell) pepper/capsicum and 1 finely chopped onion to the cooking pot as well. Once the onion has softened, add in the frozen prawns and continue as above.

Use Any Thick Curry Sauce We love this recipe with a jalfrezi sauce, but you can mix and match. Why not try Madras or tikka masala, or how about a korma? Instead of using an Indian flavour, you could also try a Thai curry sauce.

Swap the Naan If you prefer samosas, pakoras or onion bhajis, then swap these for the naan bread. Use shop-bought, already-cooked varieties and cook for 4 minutes at the same temperature.

GARLIC MUSSELS & FRITES

I'm 14 years old, sitting in my parents' motorhome in France, eating mussels and *frites*, and dunking plenty of French bread into the delicious garlic and white wine broth. It is one of my favourite foods from travelling. So, it's no surprise that when we took our own kids around France, we got the pressure cooker out to cook mussels. What my mum and I love most are the bags of prepared mussels. You can throw everything from the bag into the pot and enjoy garlic mussels in no time. Because it's traditional to serve them with fries (*frites*), we've made some fries first, then cooked the mussels.

....

SERVES **2**
FUNCTIONS **AIR FRY, SAUTÉ, PRESSURE COOK**
PREP **8 MINUTES**
AIR FRY COOK TIME **32 MINUTES**
SAUTÉ COOK TIME **5 MINUTES**
PRESSURE COOK TIME **1 MINUTE**
TOTAL COOK TIME **38 MINUTES**
CALORIES **830**

....

450g/1lb red potatoes
2 tbsp extra virgin olive oil
1 tbsp dried dill
½ tsp garlic powder
1 medium brown onion
6 garlic cloves
240ml/8½fl oz/1 cup dry white wine
1kg/2lb 4oz prepared cooked mussels (garlic sauce or white wine, or a mix), defrosted if frozen
2 tbsp roughly chopped fresh parsley
Squeeze of lemon

01 Start by preparing and cooking your fries. Scrub the potatoes and chop them into French fries – we do them a third of the thickness of our chunky chips – and place them in a bowl with 1 tablespoon of the olive oil, the dill and garlic powder. Mix well with your hands. Place the air fryer basket/crisp plate in the cooking pot and add the fries, spreading them out. Press air fry and cook at 160°C/320°F for 20 minutes. Shake and spray the fries with oil, then air fry again for another 8 minutes at the increased temperature of 180°C/360°F. Remove the air fryer basket and the fries and set aside.

02 Meanwhile, peel and finely slice the onion and garlic. Set the cooking pot to sauté, drizzle in the remaining olive oil and listen for the sizzle. Add the onion and sauté until softened. Stir in the garlic and sauté for a couple of minutes, then press cancel.

03 Deglaze the cooking pot with the white wine, then tip in the prepared mussels. Stir with a wooden spoon, then secure the pressure cooker lid, set the valve to sealing and pressure cook for 1 minute followed by a quick pressure release. Transfer the mussels to a big serving bowl, along with a sprinkling of parsley and a squeeze of lemon.

04 Place the air fryer basket/crisp plate back in the cooking pot and air fry the fries for 4 minutes at 160°C/320°F to warm them up and make them a little bit more crisp. Serve the frites with the mussels.

Steamed Mussels You can also steam the mussels, instead of using the pressure cooker. Add the mussels and the broth to the cooking pot, press steam and steam for 8 minutes.

Garlic versus White Wine Sauce I have noticed that the two main flavours available when you buy mussels are white wine and garlic. I can never choose between them, as both are delicious. We normally get a small bag of each and do both at the same time.

Creamy Seafood Sauce Mussels are often served in a creamy sauce in restaurants and there is a quick trick to making that sauce at home, after cooking the mussels and fries. Keep half of the stock from the mussels in the cooking pot, add 2 tubs (300g/10½oz) French cream cheese (we use Boursin), along with a heaped tablespoon of garlic mayonnaise, and some salt and pepper. Stir on sauté to mix well – if your cooking pot is still hot, you might not need to press sauté, as it'll heat up anyway. It thickens really well and, if you add a little extra chopped fresh parsley, it's perfect for dunking your fries in.

MIXED SEAFOOD PAELLA

My other holiday favourite, from years of travelling to Spain and from living next door in Portugal, was paella. When we lived in the Algarve, we were just a 50-minute drive across the border and the first stop was always for a paella. This recipe is easy to recreate at home.

SERVES **6**
FUNCTIONS **SAUTÉ, PRESSURE COOK**
PREP **5 MINUTES**
SAUTÉ COOK TIME **8 MINUTES**
PRESSURE COOK TIME **6 MINUTES**
TOTAL COOK TIME **14 MINUTES**
CALORIES **474**

1 medium red onion
1 red (bell) pepper/capsicum
100g/3½oz chorizo
1 tbsp extra virgin olive oil
240ml/8½fl oz/1 cup dry white wine
2 tbsp frozen chopped garlic
2 tsp turmeric
2 pinches saffron strands
960ml/34fl oz/4 cups fish
  (or vegetable) stock
500g/1lb 2oz/2 cups passata
330g/11½oz/1½ cups paella or
  arborio rice
1 × 350g/12oz pack frozen seafood
  mix (containing mussels, scallops,
  king prawns/shrimp and squid)
1 × 240g/8½oz pack frozen raw
  peeled super king prawns/shrimp
1 tbsp smoked paprika
1 tbsp dried thyme
160g/5¾oz/2 cups frozen garden
  peas
Lemon wedges, to serve
Roughly chopped fresh parsley, to
  serve

01 Peel and finely dice the onion, deseed and chop the pepper into small chunks, and slice the chorizo. Press sauté on the multicooker, and add the onion, pepper, chorizo and olive oil to the cooking pot. Wait for the sizzle, then sauté until the onion has softened.

02 Cancel sauté and deglaze the cooking pot with the white wine. Stir in the frozen garlic, turmeric and saffron. Pour in the stock and passata, followed by the rice. Give it a good stir. Gently place the frozen seafood and the prawns on top of the rice and don't stir.

03 Secure the pressure cooker lid and pressure cook for 6 minutes followed by a 10-minute natural pressure release.

04 After releasing pressure, add all the remaining ingredients and continue to stir. The sauce will thicken as you stir.

05 Serve it hot straight from the pot with lemon wedges and roughly chopped parsley.

Classic Look If you want a more yellow look (like a traditional paella), you can add extra turmeric or some yellow food colouring.

Paella Soup This is a keeper and perfect for when you have loads of leftover paella. I had roughly half of the paella left in the cooking pot, which worked out at 1.2kg/2lb 12oz. Add 720ml/25fl oz/3 cups fish stock, 120ml/4fl oz/ ½ cup white wine, some more salt and pepper, and 2 tablespoons of roughly chopped fresh parsley. If you have any spare seafood, stir that into the pot, too. If I'm adding extra seafood, it's usually an extra pack of the frozen seafood mix, as mentioned in the recipe. Complete a 0-minute pressure cook, followed by a quick pressure release, and the soup is warmed up and ready to eat.

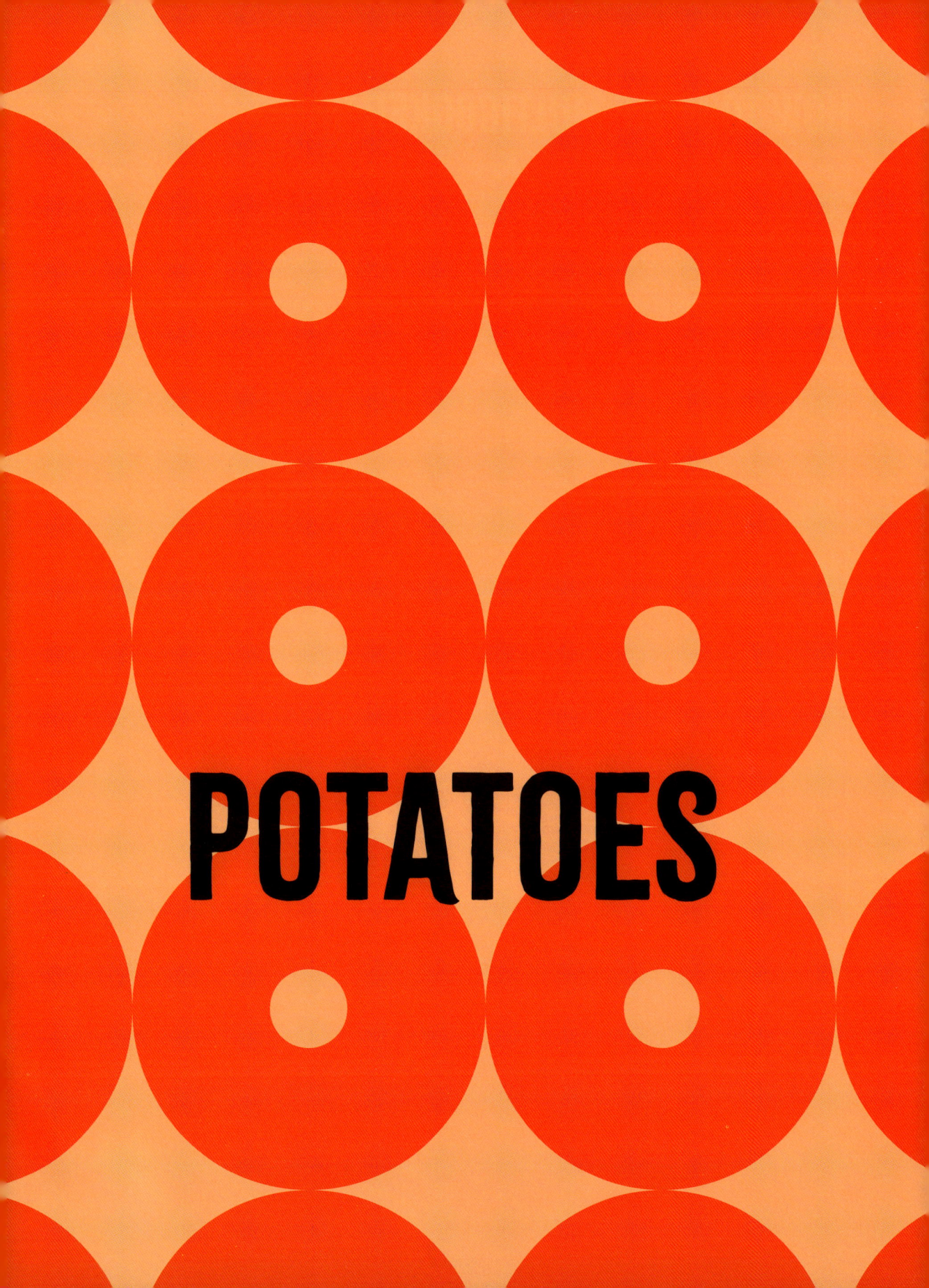

HOW TO MAKE MULTICOOKER CHIPS

If you're going to experiment with a food, it had better be one that is cheap to buy, easy to prepare, anyone can get worldwide, and will give you a lesson in the multicooker settings. I often get asked which setting I use when I make chips. Should you use air fry, bake, roast, or (with the modern multicookers) steam air fry, steam bake, or steam roast? I also get asked what to do if you want to steam air fry but you don't have that setting, which is why we've shared the pressure cook and air fry method. Because it can be overwhelming to a new multicooker owner, we thought we'd make chips with each setting, one by one, and share the time and temps for you to do the same. It's a great way to try out the different settings. Plus, you'll end up with lots of chips!

HOMEMADE CHIPS COOKING TIMES & TEMPERATURES

Air Fryer
If I just had an air fryer with lots of presets (such as, bake, chips setting, grill etc.), I would always opt for air fryer. This is because it has the fastest fans and, if you want a crispy, perfect texture to your chips, that is the setting to choose. But, to get the best results and a fluffy centre, you need to cook them at a lower temperature first.

Cooking time & temp 15 minutes at 160°C/320°F, shake the chips, then air fry for another 10 minutes at 180°C/360°F.

Bake & Roast
This was really interesting because, thanks to our air fryer dual, we could set one drawer to bake and the other to roast and compare notes. Both chips had a really fluffy centre, and we felt like there was not much difference between the two settings. Because bake and roast have slower fans, it means you need to cook the chips for longer, if you want the crispy texture.

Cooking time & temp 18 minutes at 160°C/320°F, shake the chips, then air fry for another 10 minutes at 180°C/360°F.

Pressure Cook & Air Fry
This is when chips meet the roast potato style of cooking to create delicious chip shop chips. You use the 0-minute pressure cooking time to blanch the potatoes, then pat them dry with kitchen/paper towel. Place them in a bowl with oil and seasonings, then transfer to the air fryer basket/crisp plate. Chips take 20 minutes and taste so good. Adjust the cooking depending on how crispy you like them.

Cooking time & temp 0-minute pressure cook with 240ml/8½fl oz/1 cup water followed by air fry at 180°C/360°F for 20 minutes.

Steam Air Fry
With this setting, they are steamed and air fried at the same time. This gives the fluffy centre and the crispy outside. Because it all happens in the cooking pot, you don't need to remove the chips to oil them, then return them to the pot. Although you need to follow the instructions opposite, to avoid soggy chips.

Cooking time & temp 18 minutes at 160°C/320°F and then steam air fry for 8 minutes at 180°C/360°F.

Steam Bake & Steam Roast
This is just like the bake and roast on modern air fryers; it cooks more slowly, so you get the perfect centre but the crisp is lacking. The same applies with the steam feature. This is perfect for roasting meats and root vegetables etc. but is not ideal for chips.

Cooking time & temp 25 minutes at 180°C/360°F, then leave to rest for 5 minutes before serving.

STEAM AIR FRY CHIPS

These are perfect chips using the steam air fry setting. We prepare them skin on for extra crispiness, and season with Cajun spices.

SERVES **4**
FUNCTIONS **STEAM AIR FRY**
PREP **5 MINUTES**
STEAM AIR FRY COOK TIME **26 MINUTES**
TOTAL COOK TIME **26 MINUTES**
CALORIES **155**

450g/1lb red potatoes
1 tbsp extra virgin olive oil
1 tbsp Cajun seasoning
Extra virgin olive oil spray

01 Scrub the potatoes, then slice them into medium-thick, chunky chips (known as steak fries in the US). Place the chips in a bowl with the olive oil and Cajun seasoning. Sprinkle a generous amount of salt and pepper over the top and mix everything together well with your hands, to give the chips an even coating. If you like more of a spice kick, add more Cajun seasoning.

02 Pour 240ml/8½fl oz/1 cup cold water into the bottom of the cooking pot, then add the air fryer basket/crisp plate. Tip in your potatoes and spread them out.

03 Secure the lid, press steam air fry and set the temperature to 160°C/320°F and the cooking time to 18 minutes.

04 Open the lid and, without shaking the chips, spray them with a little olive oil. Cook for a further 8 minutes at an increased temperature of 180°C/360°F. Let the chips sit in the multicooker for about 5 minutes to cool before moving them. (This stops them from sticking to the bottom of the air fryer basket/crisp plate and lets them firm up.)

Don't Have a Steam Air Fry Button? Simply use the air fryer button – there's no need to add water to the pot. Follow the same cooking time and temperature as above.

Sweet Potato Chips If you're making sweet potato chips, increase the temp to 180°C/360°F and cook for 20 minutes.

PERI PERI SWEET POTATO WEDGES

When I have lots of sweet potatoes, I can guarantee I'll be making these wedges. They are also brilliant for when sweet potatoes are out of season and you can only get those small sweet potatoes, as they are easy to cut into wedges. We have used the steam bake setting and the air fryer setting for the best of both worlds, but you could swap this for just air fry.

....

SERVES **4**
FUNCTIONS **STEAM BAKE, AIR FRY**
PREP **5 MINUTES**
STEAM BAKE COOK TIME **25 MINUTES**
AIR FRY COOK TIME **5 MINUTES**
TOTAL COOK TIME **30 MINUTES**
CALORIES **238**

....

4 small sweet potatoes
2 tbsp extra virgin olive oil
1 tsp smoked paprika
½ tsp garlic powder
2 tsp ground coriander
2 tsp peri peri salt (we use Nando's)
Extra virgin olive oil spray
Peri peri mayonnaise (we use Nando's), to serve

01 Scrub the sweet potatoes, then slice them into wedges (we find we get 4 wedges out of each small sweet potato) and place them in a large mixing bowl. Drizzle with the olive oil and add the smoked paprika, garlic powder and coriander, then mix well with your hands.

02 Pour 240ml/8½fl oz/1 cup water into the cooking pot. Place the air fryer basket/crisp plate in the cooking pot and tip in the sweet potato wedges. Use your hands to spread them out to ensure even cooking. Secure the lid, press steam bake and set the temperature to 180°C/360°F and the cooking time to 25 minutes.

03 Remove the lid and spray the tops of the wedges with a little olive oil and continue to cook for a further 5 minutes on air fry at the same temperature.

04 Transfer the wedges to a serving dish and give them a sprinkle of peri peri salt. Serve them with your favourite shop-bought peri peri mayonnaise.

White Potato Wedges You can swap the sweet potatoes for white potatoes. Use the steam bake setting, adding liquid as above, but steam bake for 20 minutes at 180°C/360°F and finish with a 3-minute air fry at 200°C/400°F to make them crisp.

Just Air Fry Wedges If you only have the air fry setting, follow the same cooking time and temperature as above but there's no need to add water, as there is no steaming required.

GARLIC & HERB ROAST POTATOES

How do you adapt the parboil and oven bake method of making roast potatoes to a multicooker? You pressure cook the potatoes first, then you use the air fryer. The result is the most amazing fluffed-up roast potatoes. Plus, this modern version of the classic has the benefit of being much faster to cook than the traditional method.

....

SERVES **6**
FUNCTIONS **PRESSURE COOK, AIR FRY**
PREP **8 MINUTES**
PRESSURE COOK TIME **0 MINUTES**
AIR FRY COOK TIME **25 MINUTES**
TOTAL COOK TIME **25 MINUTES**
CALORIES **226**

....

1.3kg/3lb white potatoes
2 tbsp extra virgin olive oil
2 tsp garlic purée
2 tsp dried rosemary
1 tsp mixed herbs/Italian seasoning

01 Place 240ml/8½fl oz/1 cup water into the cooking pot, then add your air fryer basket/crisp plate.

02 Peel and chop the potatoes. We like to make them a similar size to traditional roast potatoes by chopping the potatoes in half or, if they are very big, into quarters. Place the potatoes in the air fryer basket/crisp plate and season them generously with salt and pepper.

03 Secure the pressure cooker lid, set the valve to sealing and pressure cook for 0 minutes followed by a quick pressure release. The potatoes should be fork tender. Leave them to cool in the air fryer basket/crisp plate, as they will be easier to handle when preparing them for air frying.

04 Remove the air fryer basket/crisp plate and drain the water out of the cooking pot. Tip the potatoes into a mixing bowl, then drizzle in the olive oil. Add the garlic purée and herbs, and season generously with salt and pepper. Give the bowl a good shake, as this will help fluff up the edges of the potatoes.

05 Transfer the potatoes back into the air fryer basket/crisp plate. Using the air fryer button, set the temperature to 200°C/400°F and the cooking time to 25 minutes. Shake the basket/crisp plate a couple of times during the cooking time, so the potatoes brown evenly.

Steam Roast Add 240ml/8½fl oz/1 cup vegetable stock to the cooking pot, then set the air fryer basket/crisp plate in place. Add the prepared potatoes and steam roast for 25 minutes at 180°C/360°F. Any remaining vegetable stock can be used in your gravy.

Love Baby Potatoes Mix a bag of baby potatoes in a bowl with a tablespoon of olive oil, a tablespoon of dried basil and a generous seasoning of salt and pepper, and mix them with your hands. Add 240ml/8½fl oz/1 cup vegetable stock to the cooking pot, set the air fryer basket/crisp plate in place and add the baby potatoes. Steam roast for 20 minutes at 160°C/320°F. You'll love the crispy skins!

Same Recipe Different Fats You can swap the olive oil in this recipe for the same quantity of vegetable oil, duck fat, goose fat, or melted butter.

EGG MAYO & CRESS JACKET POTATOES

We have just shown you how to convert roast potatoes from saucepan and oven, to pressure cook and air fry, to save on cooking time. But when we make jacket potatoes, most of us microwave and oven bake. So, what would you do differently? You also pressure cook and air fry. Pressure cooking cooks the potatoes fast and helps with a fluffy centre, whilst the air fry button gives you perfectly crispy skin.

....

SERVES **4**
FUNCTIONS **PRESSURE COOK, AIR FRY,**
PREP **4 MINUTES**
PRESSURE COOK TIME **32 MINUTES**
AIR FRY COOK TIME **15 MINUTES**
TOTAL COOK TIME **47 MINUTES**
CALORIES **380**

....

4 medium baking potatoes
Extra virgin olive oil spray
2 tbsp salted butter

MAKE-AHEAD EGG MAYO
4 large eggs
2 tbsp roughly chopped fresh parsley
2 tbsp garlic mayonnaise
1 punnet cress

01 Make the egg mayo first and keep it in the fridge for later. Grease a 18cm/7in round silicone container and crack the eggs into it. Pour 240ml/8½fl oz/1 cup water into the cooking pot, add the trivet/rack in top position and place the silicone container on top. Secure the pressure cooker lid, set the valve to sealing and pressure cook for 12 minutes, followed by a quick pressure release. You will have perfectly boiled eggs without needing to peel them. Transfer the eggs to a mixing bowl and use a knife to break them up into small chunks. Add the parsley and garlic mayonnaise, and season generously with salt and pepper. Roughly chop the cress and add it to the bowl. Mix well, then place the bowl in the fridge until the potatoes are ready.

02 Add the air fryer basket/crisp plate to the cooking pot and make sure you still have 240ml/8½fl oz/1 cup water inside. Place the baking potatoes on the air fryer basket/crisp plate. Secure the pressure cooker lid, set the valve to sealing and pressure cook for 20 minutes, followed by a quick pressure release.

03 After releasing the remaining pressure, the potatoes will be fork tender and ready for air frying. Leave them until cool enough to handle.

04 Remove the air fryer basket/crisp plate and drain the water. Tip the potatoes onto a dinner plate and give them a generous seasoning of salt and pepper, followed by a good spray of olive oil. Roll them over and do the same again. Continue to roll them in the excess oil and salt and pepper on the plate, so they get a really good coating.

05 Transfer the potatoes to the air fryer basket/crisp plate and place this in the cooking pot. Secure the lid and, using the air fryer button, set the temperature to 200°C/400°F and the cooking time to 15 minutes. Turn the potatoes halfway through the cooking time, so both sides get crispy.

06 Slice the potatoes open, add the butter and load up with the egg mayo you made earlier, and any extra cress.

SAM & DOM'S FAVOURITE TOPPINGS

Baked Beans & Cheese Load up your jacket potatoes with our baked beans recipe from page 50.

Sour Cream & Bacon Sauté 200g/7oz bacon bits in the cooking pot with a tablespoon of olive oil until nice and crispy. Add them to a mixing bowl with 4 heaped tablespoons sour cream, along with 1 teaspoon dried chives. Mix well and load up your potatoes.

Steam Roast Jackets Add 240ml/8½fl oz/1 cup water to the cooking pot, place the air fryer basket/crisp plate inside and cook the baking potatoes for 40 minutes at 160°C/320°F on steam roast or steam bake.

BUBBLE & SQUEAK

The best way to eat cabbage!

SERVES **4**
FUNCTIONS **PRESSURE COOK**
PREP **10 MINUTES**
PRESSURE COOK TIME **8 MINUTES**
TOTAL COOK TIME **8 MINUTES**
CALORIES **674**

1.3kg/3lb white potatoes
1 medium Savoy cabbage
240ml/8½fl oz/1 cup vegetable stock
170g/6oz/¾ cup salted butter
2 tbsp dried parsley

01 Peel and chop the potatoes into medium chunks, then load them into the cooking pot. Roughly chop the cabbage and add it to the cooking pot with the potatoes. Give them a good stir, then pour in the stock. Add 55g/2oz of the butter, chopping it into chunks as you add it.

02 Secure the pressure cooker lid, set the valve to sealing, and pressure cook for 8 minutes followed by a quick pressure release.

03 Carefully remove the lid and drain the potatoes and cabbage from the stock. (Save the stock for another meal as it's so flavoursome.) Place the cabbage and potatoes in a bowl with the remaining butter, dried parsley and a generous seasoning of salt and pepper. Mash with a potato masher and serve.

Leftovers 101 If you have leftover cabbage from Sunday lunch, then just pressure cook the potatoes and stir in the cabbage at the end.

MUSTARD MASH

Give your mashed potatoes a make over with the addition of some mustard. This mustard mash is so creamy and is perfect for pairing with roast beef.

SERVES **4**
FUNCTIONS **PRESSURE COOK**
PREP **8 MINUTES**
PRESSURE COOK TIME **8 MINUTES**
TOTAL COOK TIME **8 MINUTES**
CALORIES **506**

1.3kg/3lb white potatoes
240ml/8½fl oz/1 cup vegetable stock
115g/4oz/½ cup salted butter
1 tbsp wholegrain mustard
1 tbsp finely chopped fresh parsley

01 Peel and chop the potatoes into medium chunks. Pour the stock into the cooking pot and add the steamer basket. Load the potato chunks into the steamer basket and add half the butter.

02 Secure the pressure cooker lid, set the valve to sealing, and pressure cook for 8 minutes followed by a quick pressure release.

03 Carefully remove the lid and drain the stock. (Save this for another meal as it's so flavoursome.) Place the potatoes in a mixing bowl with the remaining butter, the mustard, parsley and a generous seasoning of salt and pepper. Mash with a potato masher. Do a taste test and adjust with extra mustard, depending on how you like it.

Mash 101 Because the pressure cooker makes the potatoes so soft, it's effortless to make mash. Quite often I just use a fork to mash the potatoes, especially when I'm away from home without my usual kit.

ROOT VEGETABLE MASH

When root veg are on sale, batch this!

SERVES **4**
FUNCTIONS **PRESSURE COOK**
PREP **10 MINUTES**
PRESSURE COOK TIME **8 MINUTES**
TOTAL COOK TIME **8 MINUTES**
CALORIES **449**

6 large carrots
1 small swede/rutabaga
3 baking potatoes
240ml/8½fl oz/1 cup vegetable stock
115g/4oz/½ cup salted butter
1 tbsp dried parsley

01 Peel and cut the carrots, swede and potatoes into medium chunks.

02 Pour the stock into the cooking pot and add the steamer basket. Place all the root veg in the steamer. Chop half the butter into chunks and place on the vegetables.

03 Secure the pressure cooker lid, set the valve to sealing, and pressure cook for 8 minutes followed by a quick pressure release.

04 After releasing the pressure, drain the stock (save it for another meal as it's so flavoursome), then mash the vegetables in the pot with a silicone masher, adding the remaining butter a little at a time. Finish with the parsley and season generously with salt and pepper before serving.

Don't Have Swede? When root vegetables are in season, we have this mash all … the … time. It's delicious and very versatile, as you can mix and match the root vegetables, according to what you have.

CAULIFLOWER MASH

We love how quick cauliflower mash is to make with the help of the pressure cooker.

SERVES **4**
FUNCTIONS **PRESSURE COOK**
PREP **8 MINUTES**
PRESSURE COOK TIME **8 MINUTES**
TOTAL COOK TIME **8 MINUTES**
CALORIES **382**

2 large cauliflowers
240ml/8½fl oz/1 cup vegetable stock
55g/2oz/¼ cup salted butter
28g/1oz/⅓ cup grated Parmesan
1 tsp garlic purée
1 tbsp sour cream
2 tsp all-purpose seasoning

01 Break the cauliflowers into medium florets. Pour the stock into the cooking pot and add the steamer basket. Place the cauliflower in the steamer basket. Chop the butter into chunks and add to the pot with the florets.

02 Secure the pressure cooker lid and set the valve to sealing. Pressure cook for 8 minutes followed by a quick pressure release.

03 After releasing the pressure, thoroughly drain the stock (save it for another meal as it's so flavoursome), then place the cauliflower in a mixing bowl, along with all the remaining ingredients. Mash with a masher until smooth. Season generously with salt and pepper before serving.

Low-carb Mash This cauliflower mash is brilliant as a low-carb alternative to traditional mash. In any recipes in this book, such as the shepherd's pie on page 85, you can swap regular mash for this one and keep your carbs down.

DOM'S CHEESY POTATO CAKES

There is nothing more satisfying than using mash you have made previously, frozen in the freezer, then defrosted to create cheesy potato cakes. They are like a potato-only version of a fishcake but also remind me of fritters. You could load them up with other vegetable leftovers, such as cabbage, to make bubble and squeak cakes.

SERVES **8**
FUNCTIONS **AIR FRY**
PREP **6 MINUTES**
AIR FRY COOK TIME **10 MINUTES**
TOTAL COOK TIME **10 MINUTES**
CALORIES **247**

650g/1lb 7oz leftover mashed potatoes
115g/4oz cream cheese (we use Philadelphia Light)
120g/4¼oz/1¼ cups grated Parmesan
100g/3½oz/2 cups breadcrumbs (we use panko)
2 tsp dried parsley
Tomato ketchup (optional)

TOMATO SALAD
Handful iceburg lettuce
55g/2oz cherry tomatoes
Extra virgin olive oil
Balsamic vinegar

01 Place all the ingredients in a medium mixing bowl and mix well. Using your hands, make 8 equal-sized potato patties (think the shape of a flat fishcake or a fritter).

02 Place a layer of foil in the air fryer basket/crisp plate and lower this into the cooking pot. Add as many potato cakes as will fit in a single layer, then press air fry and cook at 200°C/400°F for 10 minutes, or until crispy and golden. Continue until all the patties are cooked.

03 Serve the potato cakes with a tomato salad. Slice the lettuce and quarter the cherry tomatoes, then drizzle both with olive oil and balsamic vinegar, and sprinkle with salt. The potato cakes also taste amazing with the addition of some tomato ketchup.

Freezer Mash There are many different containers in which you can freeze mash. Our favourite method uses large freezer cubes, like the ones on page 14. Just pop them out of the freezer cubes once frozen and store them in a heavy-duty freezer bag. If you are being potato-cake savvy, you could weigh the leftovers before freezing them, so you freeze the exact amount for this recipe. When freezing mash, make sure it's fully cool first, then seal the freezer container and label it for later. You could also freeze it in small ice-cube trays and use a cube of mash as a quick thickener for stews and casseroles.

Ham & Cheese Cakes We love ham in the Milner house and, if you have any ham in the fridge, you could dice it finely and add it to the potato cake mixture to make a delicious variation.

PATATAS BRAVAS CASSEROLE

My favourite dish on the tapas menu is patatas bravas. But, I wondered, what if I could make it into a one-pot dinner? With olives and chorizo, and served with crusty bread, aioli and a glass of red wine? That's how this creamy casserole was born, and it pressure cooks in just 3 minutes.

SERVES **4**
FUNCTIONS **SAUTÉ, PRESSURE COOK**
PREP **5 MINUTES**
SAUTÉ COOK TIME **8 MINUTES**
PRESSURE COOK TIME **3 MINUTES**
TOTAL COOK TIME **11 MINUTES**
CALORIES **604**

- 2 × 120g/4¼oz packs marinated mixed olives in chilli
- 2 red (bell) peppers/capsicum
- 1 medium red onion
- 130g/4½oz chorizo
- 240ml/8½fl oz/1 cup red wine
- 225g/8oz cherry tomatoes
- 900g/2lb baby potatoes
- 1 tbsp frozen chopped garlic
- 500g/1lb 2oz/2 cups passata
- 240ml/8½fl oz/1 cup vegetable stock
- 1 tbsp dried thyme
- 1 tsp crushed dried chilli flakes
- 2 tsp ground coriander
- 2 tsp smoked paprika
- 1 tbsp roughly chopped fresh coriander/cilantro
- 2 tbsp aioli, to serve

01 Press the sauté button on the multicooker. Add the olives and the oil from the pack to the cooking pot and give them a quick stir.

02 Deseed the peppers and slice them into 1cm/½in chunks, and peel and slice the onion into the same-sized chunks as the multicooker warms up. Roughly chop the chorizo. When you hear the sizzle, add the chorizo, onion and peppers, and sauté until the onion has softened.

03 Cancel sauté, pour in the wine and deglaze the cooking pot, scraping the bottom with a wooden spoon.

04 Chop all the cherry tomatoes and baby potatoes in half, and add them to the pot (cut the potatoes in quarters, if they are particularly large). Stir in the frozen garlic, passata, stock and dried thyme. Sprinkle in the chilli flakes, ground coriander and smoked paprika, and give the casserole a good stir.

05 Secure the pressure cooker lid and set the valve to sealing. Pressure cook for 3 minutes, followed by a quick pressure release.

06 Carefully remove the lid and stir the casserole, adding half the chopped coriander, and seasoning generously with salt and pepper.

07 Using a stick blender, blend about 5 potatoes and stir them into the sauce to make it nice and creamy, then serve straight from the pot with the aioli and the remaining coriander, some crusty bread and a drizzle of olive oil. And don't forget your glass of red wine!

The Spicy Spanish Sauce for Everything Whilst I love this chunky casserole, what is equally amazing is when it is blended until smooth. This then tastes like a delicious, creamy yet spicy tomato sauce. If you need stock for a rice or pasta dish, mix this sauce with water, in a ratio of 240ml/8½fl oz/1 cup sauce to 480ml/17fl oz/2 cups water, then mix well and use that. Delicious!

VEGETABLES

HOW TO PRESSURE COOK FROZEN VEGETABLES

We got our first electric pressure cooker on 25 November 2016. I can remember the exact date because it was Sofia's second birthday and Jorge was just a couple of months old. It was perfect timing, as we needed to be able to cook food quickly and, of course, provide a toddler with puréed veggies quickly.

That night with the kids fast asleep in bed, Dom cooked our first pressure cooker food and it was broccoli. We couldn't get over how green the broccoli looked compared to boiling and we vowed never to put a vegetable in a pan of boiling water again. Almost a decade later, we still haven't.

Fresh or frozen vegetables are brilliant in the pressure cooker. You can transform them into a soup very easily, or just serve them as a side for dinner. We recommend starting with a bag of frozen vegetables, as below, in order to see what a good job the multicooker does at pressure cooking.

A BAG OF FROZEN VEGETABLES

On page 141 we show you how to make vegetable soup from frozen vegetables. Nothing complicated – just a bag of frozen veg and some stock. But before we turned those veg into soup, it started as this bag of frozen veg.

SERVES **4**
FUNCTIONS **PRESSURE COOK**
PREP **2 MINUTES**
PRESSURE COOK TIME **0 MINUTES**
TOTAL COOK TIME **0 MINUTE**
CALORIES **96**

- 240ml/8½fl oz/1 cup vegetable stock
- 1 × 800g/1lb 12oz bag frozen vegetables (we use broccoli, carrots, cauliflower, green beans and garden peas)

01 Pour the stock into the cooking pot, then add the steamer basket. Tip the bag of frozen vegetables into the steamer basket.

02 Secure the lid on the multicooker, set the valve to sealing and pressure cook for 0 minutes, followed by a quick pressure release.

03 After you have released the pressure, season the vegetables with salt and pepper, and serve.

Triple the Liquid To turn this into the base for a soup or stew, just triple the liquid. Instead of adding 240ml/8½fl oz/1 cup liquid to the cooking pot, add 720ml/25fl oz/3 cups. This is what we do for the veg soup on page 141.

RINSE & REPEAT WITH OTHER FROZEN VEGETABLES

You can pressure cook your frozen vegetables either positioned in your air fryer basket/crisp plate, or steamer basket. As with the frozen mixed veg opposite, add the frozen vegetables and follow the cooking times below. Choose from the following veg, cooking as much as you like – up to 1kg/2lb 4oz – keeping to the cooking times below.

Broccoli florets 0 minutes

Brussels sprouts, whole 2 minutes

Butternut squash, cubed 2 minutes

Carrots (Chantenay) 5 minutes

Carrots, peeled and sliced 3 minutes

Cauliflower florets 0 minutes

Corn on the cob/cobettes 10 minutes

Garden peas 0 minutes

Green beans 0 minutes

Sweetcorn 0 minutes

White cabbage, shredded 0 minutes

WE LOVE PRESSURE COOKED FROZEN VEG

With a busy life, it's very easy to end up with changed plans and the broccoli you bought for dinner tonight or those green beans you meant to cook tomorrow get forgotten about and quickly lose their freshness. With frozen vegetables, though, you don't have to worry – they are frozen when they are at their best. Because they are blanched just before being frozen, they cook much more quickly in your kitchen gadgets, too, and this makes mealtimes faster. You can grab just what you need, or do a medley, as we have done opposite. We also find that the broccoli in particular is better cooked from frozen with the air fryer than fresh.

CREAMED CABBAGE & LEEKS

On a busy weeknight, we love a quick shortcut. Cabbage and leeks with garlic and cream cheese - bring it on!

SERVES **4**
FUNCTIONS **PRESSURE COOK, SAUTÉ**
PREP **5 MINUTES**
PRESSURE COOK TIME **0 MINUTES**
SAUTÉ COOK TIME **5 MINUTES**
TOTAL COOK TIME **5 MINUTES**
CALORIES **151**

240ml/8½fl oz/1 cup vegetable stock
1 × 300g/10½oz bag shredded cabbage/leeks
1 × 165g/5¾oz tub cream cheese (we use Philadelphia Light)
2 tsp garlic purée
1 tbsp mixed herbs/Italian seasoning

01 Pour the stock into the cooking pot. Add the steamer basket and tip in the shredded veg.

02 Secure the pressure cooker lid, set the valve to sealing and pressure cook for 0 minutes, followed by a quick pressure release. Carefully remove the lid, and set aside the steamer basket with the just-cooked veg still inside.

03 Press sauté and add the cream cheese to the remaining stock in the cooking pot. Add the garlic purée and stir with a wooden spoon until you have a creamy sauce consistency. Cancel the sauté.

04 Tip the veg back into the cooking pot, add the mixed herbs and a generous seasoning of salt and pepper. Stir well before serving.

Mix & Match the Veg You can make this with just cabbage, or swap the cabbage for spring greens, or why not cook it with kale instead?

CREAMY WILTED SPINACH

I love spinach and this is how to make it using the steam function.

SERVES **1**
FUNCTIONS **STEAM**
PREP **4 MINUTES**
STEAM COOK TIME **2 MINUTES**
TOTAL COOK TIME **2 MINUTES**
CALORIES **268**

240ml/8½fl oz/1 cup vegetable stock
1 × 160g/5¾oz bag baby spinach
2 tbsp salted butter

01 Pour the stock into the cooking pot and add the air fryer basket/crisp plate. Tip the spinach into the air fryer basket/crisp plate. Dot the top with the butter, cutting it into small chunks as you go, and season generously with salt and pepper.

02 Secure the lid and set it to steam for 2 minutes, or until the spinach has wilted.

03 Give it a good stir and wonder to yourself where all the spinach has gone before serving!

Spinach Pasta Bake Next time you fancy spinach pasta bake, mix this wilted spinach with a small tub of ricotta and it will make the most wonderful sauce.

GARLIC ROASTED FENNEL

I love the taste of fennel. This is how to use the steam roast function to cook fennel, speeding it up when compared to how long it would take in the oven.

SERVES **2**
FUCNTIONS **STEAM ROAST**
PREP **4 MINUTES**
STEAM ROAST TIME **8 MINUTES**
TOTAL COOK TIME **8 MINUTES**
CALORIES **92**

2 fennel bulbs
240ml/8½fl oz/1 cup vegetable stock
Extra virgin olive oil spray
1 tsp garlic powder

01 Quarter each fennel bulb lengthways.

02 Pour the stock into the cooking pot and add the air fryer basket/crisp plate. Place the fennel wedges into the air fryer basket/crisp plate and spray them with olive oil. Sprinkle over the garlic powder and season with salt and pepper.

03 Secure the multicooker lid and set it to steam roast at 180°C/360°F for 8 minutes, or until the fennel is done to your liking.

Love Chinese Fennel Having a Chinese and want a quick side dish? Follow this recipe but add 2 teaspoons Chinese five spice to the fennel.

CRISPY CURRIED KALE

This is our favourite healthy air fryer snack, as it goes perfectly crispy every time.

SERVES **2**
FUNCTIONS **STEAM AIR FRY**
PREP **4 MINUTES**
STEAM AIR FRY TIME **5 MINUTES**
TOTAL COOK TIME **5 MINUTES**
CALORIES **99**

85g/3oz curly kale
1 tbsp extra virgin olive oil
2 tsp ground cumin
1 tsp garam masala
240ml/8½fl oz/1 cup vegetable stock

01 Remove any tough stalks from the kale and give it a good wash. Drain it well, then dab it dry with kitchen towel/paper towel and place it in a mixing bowl with the olive oil, cumin, garam masala and salt and pepper. Mix everything together with your hands.

02 Pour the stock into the cooking pot and add the air fryer basket/crisp plate. Place the kale in the air fryer basket/crisp plate and spread it out.

03 Secure the lid of the multicooker and set it to steam air fry at 180°C/360°F for 5 minutes, or until crispy to your liking.

Mix & Match the Seasoning You can swap the cumin and garam masala for 1 tablespoon of any dried seasoning. We love it with fajita seasoning for our Friday night movie night.

FENNEL & THYME HASSELBACK CARROTS

This is my favourite way to cook carrots in the multicooker.

SERVES **2**
FUNCTIONS **STEAM ROAST, GRILL/BROIL**
PREP **8 MINUTES**
STEAM ROAST COOK TIME **20 MINUTES**
GRILL COOK TIME **3 MINUTES**
TOTAL COOK TIME **23 MINUTES**
CALORIES **246**

8 medium carrots
2 tbsp extra virgin olive oil
1 tsp garlic powder
1 tbsp dried thyme
2 tsp fennel seeds
1 tbsp balsamic vinegar

01 Peel the carrots, then use a sharp knife to transform them into hasselbacks. Slice each carrot in intervals, taking the knife three-quarters of the way down, so that the carrot is still joined at the base. Place all the carrots in a bowl and add the olive oil, garlic powder, and half the thyme and fennel seeds. Season generously with salt and pepper. Mix them well with your hands, but be careful, as you don't want to break the hasselbacks.

02 Pour 240ml/8½fl oz/1 cup water into the cooking pot and add the air fryer basket/crisp plate. Tip in the carrots.

03 Secure the lid of the multicooker and set it to steam roast at 170°C/340°F for 20 minutes.

04 Carefully transfer the carrots back into the mixing bowl and add the remaining thyme and fennel seeds, as well as the balsamic vinegar. Shake the bowl gently to coat the carrots evenly, but avoid touching them as they will be hot. Be careful not to break them.

05 Return the carrots to the air fryer basket/crisp plate and set it to grill/broil for 3 minutes at 240°C/465°F, to crisp up and give them a golden glow.

ASPARAGUS BUNDLES WRAPPED IN BACON

Asparagus is another favourite veg of mine to cook in the multicooker. You could air fry or steam air fry.

SERVES **2**
FUNCTIONS **STEAM AIR FRY**
PREP **5 MINUTES**
STEAM AIR FRY COOK TIME **8 MINUTES**
TOTAL COOK TIME **8 MINUTES**
CALORIES **253**

16 asparagus spears (about 2 packs)
4 rashers back bacon/lean bacon
4 tsp cream cheese (we use Philadelphia Light)

01 Remove the woody ends from the asparagus. Place the slices of bacon on a chopping board. Arrange 4 asparagus spears on each rasher and season them with salt and pepper. Spread a teaspoon of cream cheese on each asparagus bundle. (The cheese will help the bacon stick to the asparagus and will stop the bundle coming apart as it steam air fries.) Wrap the bacon tightly around the asparagus. Continue to make 4 asparagus bundles.

02 Pour 240ml/8½fl oz/1 cup water into the cooking pot and add the air fryer basket/crisp plate. Place the asparagus and bacon bundles in the air fryer basket/crisp plate and secure the lid. Set it to steam air fry at 160°C/320°F for 8 minutes.

03 Serve them warm.

Just Air Frying If you just want to air fry, cook them for 8 minutes at the higher temperature of 200°C/400°F to get the best result.

On the Grill You could grill/broil the bundles for 8 minutes at 240°C/465°F.

HONEY GLAZED PARSNIPS

This is another great way of combining pressure cooking and air frying for a fast and delicious result. No matter how many times we cook our roast parsnips like this, we can't believe how quickly they are ready.

SERVES **6**
FUNCTIONS **PRESSURE COOK, AIR FRY**
PREP **8 MINUTES**
PRESSURE COOK TIME **0 MINUTES**
AIR FRY COOK TIME **25 MINUTES**
TOTAL COOK TIME **25 MINUTES**
CALORIES **133**

3 large parsnips

HONEY GLAZE
2 tbsp extra virgin olive oil
1 tbsp garlic purée
2 tbsp clear honey
1 tbsp roughly chopped fresh parsley

01 Peel and slice the parsnips. Depending on how big they are, we will either slice them in thirds lengthways, or in half horizontally, then cut the thin end in half lengthways and the fat end into quarters.

02 Pour 240ml/8½fl oz/1 cup water into the cooking pot and add the air fryer basket/crisp plate. Tip the parsnips into the air fryer basket/crisp plate.

03 Secure the pressure cooker lid, set the valve to sealing and pressure cook for 0 minutes, followed by a quick pressure release. The parsnips will now be fork tender and ready for air frying. Remove the air fryer basket, drain the water and let the parsnips cool for 20 minutes, or until the air fryer basket is cool enough to touch.

04 Meanwhile, place the honey glaze ingredients in a bowl and mix well with a dessertspoon.

05 Tip the cooked parsnips into the bowl with the glaze and season generously with salt and pepper. Give the bowl and good shake to fluff up the edges of the parsnips. Transfer the parsnips back to the air fryer basket.

06 Using the air fryer button, set the temperature to 200°C/400°F and the cooking time to 15 minutes. Shake them a couple of times, to encourage them to go brown evenly from the honey, then cook them at the same temperature for another 10 minutes, or until they are your preferred level of crispiness.

Steam Roast Prepare the parsnips with the honey, add 240ml/8½fl oz/1 cup liquid to the cooking pot and the air fryer basket/crisp plate. Steam roast for 25 minutes at 180°C/360°F. Turn them over for the last 10 minutes for an even glaze.

VEGETABLE STEW WITH CHEESY DUMPLINGS

This is a throw-it-all-in-the-slow-cooker dish. Just add some cheesy dumplings and you have a vegetarian version of a stew and dumplings. This recipe came about because I had too many root vegetables. We lived in Portugal back then and couldn't get suet for dumplings unless you wanted to pay the crazy prices. It's one of those recipes that you make out of necessity, but then fall in love with.

SERVES **6**
FUNCTIONS **SLOW COOK**
PREP **12 MINUTES**
SLOW COOK TIME **4½ HOURS**
TOTAL COOK TIME **4½ HOURS**
CALORIES **648**

3 large carrots
6 large potatoes
3 medium parsnips
2 leeks
1 medium swede/rutabaga
2 tbsp dried oregano
2 tbsp dried thyme
960ml/34fl oz/4 cups vegetable stock
Chopped chives, for sprinkling

CHEESY DUMPLINGS
175g/6oz/1¼ cups self-raising/self-rising flour
28g/1oz salted butter
85g/3oz/1 cup grated Parmesan
1 tbsp dried chives
1 large egg
4 tbsp whole/full-fat milk

01 Prepare all the vegetables. Clean, peel and dice them, then load them into the cooking pot. I like my vegetables to be 2cm/¾in cubes, but it's personal choice. Once they are all in the cooking pot, add the oregano and thyme, and season generously with salt and pepper. Pour in the stock and mix well with a wooden spoon.

02 Secure the lid on the multicooker (this might need to be the pressure cooker lid but don't set to sealing) and slow cook for 3 hours on high, or 5 hours on low.

03 Meanwhile, make the dumplings. It's often easier to make these ahead and keep them in the fridge until you need them. Place the flour and butter in a medium-large mixing bowl and use your fingertips to rub the fat into the flour until it resembles coarse breadcrumbs. Add the Parmesan, chives and a generous seasoning of salt and pepper. Crack in the egg and mix it with a fork, until the egg is incorporated. In a jug, combine the milk with 80ml/2¾fl oz/⅓ cup water, then pour this into the bowl and continue to mix. When it becomes too difficult to mix with a fork, use your hands. Dust them with flour and dust the work top, then tip the dough out. Use your hands to knead the dough lightly until you have a soft dumpling dough.

04 Shape the dough into the size of a thick pizza, then divide it into 6 pieces. Cut each piece in half to make 12. Roll each piece of dough into a dumpling shape, then arrange them on a plate until needed.

05 When the slow cooker has completed 3 hours (or 5 on low), stir the vegetables, then use a stick blender to blitz some of the veg (this will make the sauce lovely and thick without needing to add any thickeners). Arrange the dumplings on top of the stew, then put the slow cooker back on for an extra 90 minutes on high. Alternatively, you can cook your dumplings faster using the grill/broiler (as we have done in the photo – explained below).

06 Serve the stew and dumplings with a sprinkling of fresh chives.

Grilled/Broiled Dumplings Place the dumplings on the slow-cooked stew, press grill/broil and cook at 240°C/465°F for 10 minutes. The grill cooks the dumplings faster than slow cooking, and it gives them a lovely crispy texture.

Fast Pressure Cooker This vegetable stew and dumplings is a classic slow cook (4 hours on high). However, if you want to make it more quickly, you can cook the vegetable stew element for just 5 minutes with a quick pressure release in the pressure cooker. Add the dumplings and cook again on high pressure for 0 minutes.

SOUP

HOW TO PRESSURE COOK SOUP

In the Milner house, we've taken our pressure cookers and multicookers to some amazing places. It's a great way to save money when you're travelling and my go-to recipe always seems to be soup – or soup plus some locally shop-bought garlic bread!

We love to pressure cook a soup because you can make just a small portion for two, or scale it up to batch cook for the freezer. It is so easy in the pressure cooker. You just combine: vegetables + stock + pressure cook + season = soup. Use a stick blender to make it smooth or leave that step out to keep it chunky.

On page 148 we show you how to combine French onion soup, using the pressure cooker, with garlic cheese bread in the air fryer, but first let me show you how easy it is to make soup with the pressure cooker function. We begin the chapter with a no-prep creamy vegetable soup made using frozen vegetables. It's an easy start with a small ingredients list and it cooks so quickly.

As it's the world's favourite, we've also included a butternut squash soup, which is delicious and creamy. The ingredients are loaded into the multicooker, it is set tell you know it's done. Try all our vegetable soups, then get excited about the lentil soup with bacon . . .

TOP TIPS

Prefer a Creamy, Chunky Soup? Use your stick blender to blitz part of the soup, then stir it well. The blended bits create a beautiful, creamy texture, whilst chunky bits still remain. If you're making a soup to feed 6 people, aim to blend the equivalent of a ladleful of the soup.

Season Before or After? This is a question that is often asked when making multicooker soups. Pressure cooking naturally dulls the flavour, so you could add a lot of seasoning before pressure cooking. Otherwise, just season afterwards.

But I'm Not Pressure Cooking If you're not using the pressure cooker function you can season first, but it can depend. For example, if I'm making a slow cooker soup, I often add some seasoning at the start. However, with an air fryer soup, I find it easier to season at the end when I'm blending.

Love Croutons If you love croutons to dunk into your soup, don't forget to make a batch – try our recipe on page 201.

Reduce & Croutons Love croutons but don't want your soup getting cold? Use a tall trivet, or the rack in the top position, add the croutons and air fry for 3 minutes at 180°C/360°F. This will not only make delicious croutons, but will also reduce the soup.

Make a Cobb Soup Bowl I love the Australian favourite – a bread soup bowl. Using our tear and share bread on page 203, remove the filling to create a soup bowl. Pour in your soup and serve it in the bread bowl. You can also reheat the soup in the bowl at 150°C/300°F on bake for 15 minutes.

Cooking Times Know How If you'd like to use vegetables not included in this chapter just remember:

  Non-starchy 1–4 mins

  Starchy 5–10 mins

And if you're using dried beans, expect a cooking time of 35–45 minutes.

If you overcook your pressure cooker soup by a couple of minutes, it will still taste good and will blend better, but it won't be great if you want a chunky soup.

NO-PREP CREAMY VEGETABLE SOUP

On page 128 we showed you how to get started with the pressure cooker by steaming frozen vegetables. Now let's transform those no-prep veg into a delicious, creamy vegetable soup. It's so delicious you would never know it started as a cheap bag of frozen veg. It's also a perfect quick soup for after the school run. And you'll love our secret ingredient – but don't tell the kids!

SERVES 4
FUNCTIONS PRESSURE COOK
PREP 3 MINUTES
PRESSURE COOK TIME 2 MINUTES
TOTAL COOK TIME 2 MINUTES
CALORIES 197

1 × 800g/1lb 12oz bag frozen vegetables (we use broccoli, carrots, cauliflower, green beans, garden peas)
720ml/25fl oz/3 cups vegetable stock
1 tbsp heaped frozen chopped garlic
1 tbsp heaped frozen chopped rosemary
Handful bread crusts
3 tbsp thick Greek yoghurt

01 Tip the bag of frozen vegetables into the cooking pot and pour in the stock. Give it a quick stir with a wooden spoon, then sprinkle over a teaspoon each of the garlic and the rosemary.

02 Secure the pressure cooker lid and set the valve to sealing. Pressure cook for 2 minutes, followed by a quick pressure release.

03 After releasing the pressure, remove approximately 2 ladlefuls of the vegetables and set aside. Add the remaining garlic and rosemary to the pot, as well as a generous seasoning of salt and pepper.

04 Break up the crusty bits of French stick or whatever else you have. We always use Sofia's crusts that she hasn't eaten. Add the bread to the cooking pot and use a stick blender to blitz the soup until smooth.

05 Stir in the Greek yoghurt and the reserved vegetables (this gives the soup a slightly chunky texture) and serve. Smile as you eat, knowing you've got the kids eating their crusts!

Leftover Bread We love to save up leftover crusts and any other uneaten bread and freeze it in a freezer bag. There is often some of the tear and share bread (see page 203) left over from the bottom of the pot, too. We use this to thicken soups, to make breadcrumbs for breaded fish and for making croutons.

BUTTERNUT SQUASH & SWEET POTATO SOUP

It's been more than 20 years since I made my first-ever cream of butternut squash soup. I find it works beautifully with sweet potato, too, and we've included a double dose of coriander. We've served this with croutons from page 201.

SERVES **6**
FUNCTIONS **PRESSURE COOK**
PREP **12 MINUTES**
PRESSURE COOK TIME **5 MINUTES**
TOTAL COOK TIME **5 MINUTES**
CALORIES **218**

6 medium carrots
1 large sweet potato
900g/2lb butternut squash, peeled and cubed (prepared weight)
720ml/25fl oz/3 cups vegetable stock
1 tbsp garlic purée
1 tbsp ground coriander
2 tbsp roughly chopped fresh coriander/cilantro
Extra virgin olive oil, for drizzling

01 Peel and dice the carrots and sweet potato.

02 Add the carrots, sweet potato and butternut squash to the cooking pot. Pour in the stock.

03 Secure the pressure cooker lid and set the valve to sealing. Pressure cook for 5 minutes, followed by a quick pressure release.

04 After releasing the pressure, add the garlic purée, the ground and fresh coriander, and a generous seasoning of salt and pepper. Use a stick blender to blitz the soup until smooth (or until mostly smooth, if you prefer some chunks).

05 Drizzle with some olive oil just before serving with croutons from page 201.

CREAMY BROCCOLI CHEDDAR SOUP

On holiday in Florida with just a microwave to make dinner, I had to be creative. Our American readers told us to try a famous brand of broccoli cheese soup from the supermarket, so there I was warming up soup and transferring it into coffee cups. It was creamy, had lots of cheese, broccoli and carrots, and the kids kept going back for seconds. Back home, it was the first recipe I wanted to recreate from our travels and we made it again and again.

....

SERVES **6**
FUNCTIONS **SAUTÉ, PRESSURE COOK**
PREP **8 MINUTES**
SAUTÉ COOK TIME **3 MINUTES**
PRESSURE COOK TIME **1 MINUTE**
TOTAL COOK TIME **4 MINUTES**
CALORIES **306**

....

- 1 tbsp extra virgin olive oil, plus extra for drizzling
- 1 medium brown onion
- 4 medium carrots
- 5 garlic cloves
- 960ml/34fl oz/4 cups vegetable stock
- 2 medium broccoli
- 115g/4oz/1 cup grated mature/sharp Cheddar
- 2 tbsp roughly chopped fresh basil
- 2 tsp wholegrain mustard
- 4 tsp sweet paprika
- 2 tsp red (bell) pepper flakes
- 120ml/4fl oz/½ cup crème fraîche

01 Drizzle the olive oil into the cooking pot and press sauté. As it warms up, peel and roughly slice the onion, peel and chop the carrots into batons, and peel and thinly slice the garlic.

02 When you hear the sizzle, add the onion and carrots, and sauté until the onion has softened. Press cancel and add the garlic. Stir with a wooden spoon and the heat from the pot will sauté the garlic.

03 Pour the stock in the cooking pot to deglaze. Add the broccoli and place it on top of the soup ingredients without stirring, spreading it out across the surface.

04 Secure the pressure cooker lid and set the valve to sealing. Pressure cook for 1 minute, followed by a quick pressure release.

05 When releasing the pressure, remove some of the broccoli and carrots, if you want some texture in the finished soup, and set it aside.

06 Add the cheese, basil, mustard, sweet paprika, red pepper flakes and a generous seasoning of salt and pepper to the cooking pot and mix well. Stir in the crème fraîche. Use a stick blender to blitz until smooth.

07 Add the reserved broccoli and carrots, and stir. We like to serve ours with chopped basil and a drizzle of crème fraîche and olive oil.

Build Your Own Multicooker Soup This recipe uses carrots and broccoli with vegetable stock and crème fraîche. Most soups are a variation on these key ingredients. You can mix it up to suit what you have in and build your own – swap broccoli and carrots for butternut squash, sweet potato or pumpkin, and swap crème fraîche for cream, Greek yoghurt, coconut milk or even cream cheese. Aim for a good balance between root vegetables and non-starchy vegetables, though, as you don't want a watery soup that tastes like dish water!

MY MUM'S SUPER-SLIMMING CHUNKY SOUP

If you were a member of a diet club in the 1990s, the chances are you made a huge batch of vegetable soup each week. You hoped it would repair the damage that big curry you had the night before might have caused! I can remember my mum making it. It is oil free, traditionally loaded with 7 vegetables and flavoured with your favourite dried herbs and spices. We've made it even better by swapping the canned tomatoes for salsa. For us naughty parents, it can also be turned into a hidden-veg pasta sauce. Use it in any recipes in this book that call for pasta sauce jars.

SERVES **12**
FUNCTIONS **PRESSURE COOK**
PREP **8 MINUTES**
PRESSURE COOK TIME **5 MINUTES**
TOTAL COOK TIME **5 MINUTES**
CALORIES **119**

1 medium brown onion
450g/1lb medium carrots
3 celery sticks
2 medium courgettes/zucchini
2 red (bell) peppers/capsicum
10 medium tomatoes
720ml/25fl oz/3 cups vegetable stock
900g/2lb butternut squash, peeled and cubed (prepared weight)
300g/10½oz/1 cup oil-free salsa dip
2 tbsp roughly chopped fresh parsley
2 tbsp any dried spice blend (we used taco seasoning)
Fresh basil, chopped, to serve

01 Peel and dice the onion and carrots. Clean and slice the celery. Trim and slice the courgettes and peppers into medium chunks, then quarter the tomatoes.

02 Pour the stock into the cooking pot. Add the prepared veg and the squash, and pour the salsa over the top. Refill the salsa jar with water, shake it and add this, too. Give it all a stir.

03 Secure the pressure cooker lid, set the valve to sealing and cook for 5 minutes, followed by a quick pressure release.

04 Carefully remove the lid when the remaining pressure has been released, and add a generous seasoning of salt and pepper. Stir in the parsley and your preferred spice blend.

05 Using a stick blender, blitz some of the soup for a creamy chunky texture or blitz completely for a smooth soup.

06 Serve the soup with a sprinkling of chopped basil.

Prepare-ahead Butternut Squash We find that butternut squash can take up to 10 minutes to peel and dice, depending on how big it is. To save time, we often buy a few large squash when they are on offer, peel and dice them all, then use some of the cubes in soups like this one, and freeze any leftovers.

20-MINUTE FRENCH ONION SOUP

This is a favourite of ours and makes use of lots of the functions of the multicooker - sauté for the onions, pressure cook for the soup, and air fry, of course, for the garlic and cheese toasts. It's one of those soups that you'll wish you made more often.

SERVES **4**
FUNCTIONS **SAUTÉ, PRESSURE COOK, AIR FRY**
PREP **8 MINUTES**
SAUTÉ COOK TIME **8 MINUTES**
PRESSURE COOK TIME **8 MINUTES**
AIR FRY COOK TIME **4 MINUTES**
TOTAL COOK TIME **20 MINUTES**
CALORIES **418**

ONION SOUP
4 large brown onions
4 tbsp extra virgin olive oil
3 garlic cloves, thinly sliced
240ml/8½fl oz/1 cup red wine
960ml/34fl oz/4 cups beef stock
4 tsp dried thyme

GARLIC CHEESE TOASTS
½ tsp Dijon mustard
½ tsp lemon juice
1 tsp dried thyme
1 tbsp garlic mayonnaise (we use aioli)
1 tbsp light mayonnaise
⅓ French bread stick, cut into 3cm/1¼in slices
55g/2oz/½ cup Gruyère cheese, grated

01 Peel and thinly slice the onions, then tip them into the cooking pot. Add the olive oil and turn on sauté. Once you hear the sizzle, start stirring to sauté the onions. Have some patience, as you want the onions nice and caramelised for the best flavour. Continue for about 8 minutes.

02 Cancel sauté and add the garlic, stirring the pot and letting the heat from the sauté make it nice and golden really quickly.

03 Deglaze the cooking pot with the red wine, then pour in the stock. Give it a good stir.

04 Secure the pressure cooker lid and set the time to 8 minutes, followed by a quick pressure release.

05 Meanwhile, prepare the garlic cheese toasts. In a small bowl, combine the mustard, lemon juice, thyme and the two mayonnaises, then mix well with a spoon. Spread the mixture over the slices of bread, then top with the grated cheese, pushing it down lightly onto the garlic mayonnaise, to help prevent the cheese from flying off in the air fryer later. Set aside until needed.

06 Carefully remove the lid when the remaining pressure has been released. Add a generous seasoning of salt and pepper, along with the dried thyme, and give it a good stir. Add the tall trivet/rack and carefully place the garlic cheese toasts onto the tall trivet/rack in top position. Secure the air fryer lid and air fry at 180°C/360°F for 4 minutes, or until the cheese is melted and the bread is toasted to your liking.

07 Serve the onion soup with the garlic cheese toasts.

SLOW-COOKED LEEK & POTATO SOUP

My all-time favourite slow cooker soup is a leek and potato. It's one of those greats that requires minimal effort and you can just leave the mulitcooker to it. It's also perfect for the freezer if you make too much.

SERVES **6**
FUNCTIONS **SAUTÉ, SLOW COOK**
PREP **10 MINUTES**
SAUTÉ COOK TIME **5 MINUTES**
SLOW COOK TIME **4 HOURS**
TOTAL COOK TIME **4 HOURS AND 5 MINUTES**
CALORIES **322**

2 leeks
1 medium brown onion
1.3kg/3lb white potatoes
1 tbsp extra virgin olive oil, plus extra for drizzling
2 tbsp mixed herbs/Italian seasoning
1.4l/47fl oz/6 cups vegetable stock
1 tbsp garlic purée
4 bay leaves
2 tbsp salted butter
1 tbsp dried thyme
1 tbsp dried rosemary
2 tsp ground coriander
3 tbsp crème fraîche

01 Clean and slice the leeks, peel and slice the onion, and peel and chop the potatoes into medium chunks.

02 Add the leeks and onion to the cooking pot with the olive oil. Press sauté and, when you hear the sizzle, sauté until the onion has softened.

03 Cancel sauté and add the potato chunks, sprinkle in the mixed herbs and a generous seasoning of salt and pepper. Stir everything with a wooden spoon, then pour in the stock and add the garlic purée. Add the bay leaves and butter, chopping it into chunks as you place it on top.

04 Secure the multicooker lid and slow cook on high for 4 hours or until the potatoes are fork tender and soft enough to blend. (There's no need to set the valve to sealing.)

05 Discard the bay leaves, add the dried thyme and rosemary, and the coriander, along with the crème fraîche and, using a stick blender, blitz until smooth. Check the seasoning and serve with a drizzle of olive oil.

BIG BATCH BACON & LENTIL SOUP

SERVES **8**
FUNCTIONS **SAUTÉ, PRESSURE COOK**
PREP **12 MINUTES**
SAUTÉ COOK TIME **6 MINUTES**
PRESSURE COOK TIME **5 MINUTES**
TOTAL COOK TIME **11 MINUTES**
CALORIES **326**

....

4 rashers smoked back bacon
2 tbsp extra virgin olive oil
1 medium brown onion
1.4l/47fl oz/6 cups vegetable stock
4 celery sticks
5 medium carrots
4 baking potatoes
200g/7oz/1 cup dried lentil soup mix
1 tbsp garlic purée
2 tbsp mixed herbs/Italian seasoning
2 tsp fresh thyme leaves
8 tsp bacon bits (see page 158)
Fresh thyme leaves (optional)

01 Press sauté and, as the multicooker warms up, slice the bacon into small pieces. Add the bacon to the cooking pot along with half the olive oil and sauté until the bacon is cooked but not crispy.

02 Meanwhile, peel and dice the onion. Add this to the pot with the remaining olive oil. Continue sautéing.

03 Once the onions have softened, press cancel and deglaze the pot with the stock. Make sure you scrape any bits stuck to the bottom with a silicone spatula or wooden spoon.

04 Trim and finely chop the celery, peel and slice the carrots and cut the potatoes into 2cm/¾in chunks. Add them to the pot, sprinkle the dried lentil mix over the other ingredients and, using the back of a spatula, press it down so it's partly submerged in the liquid. Don't stir.

05 Secure the pressure cooker lid and set the valve to sealing. Pressure cook for 5 minutes, followed by a quick pressure release.

06 After releasing the pressure, add the garlic purée, mixed herbs, fresh thyme and a generous seasoning of salt and pepper. Give it a good stir.

07 Serve warm with crispy bacon bits. We like to sprinkle some fresh thyme over the top, too.

TACO MIXED BEAN SOUP

SERVES **4**
FUNCTIONS **PRESSURE COOK**
PREP **3 MINUTES**
PRESSURE COOK TIME **45 MINUTES**
TOTAL COOK TIME **45 MINUTES**
CALORIES **411**

....

95g/3¼oz/½ cup dried kidney beans
100g/3½oz/½ cup dried haricot beans
95g/3¼oz/½ cup dried black beans
90g/3oz/½ cup dried chickpeas
960ml/34fl oz/4 cups vegetable stock
3 × 300g/10½oz jars oil-free salsa dip
1 × 30g/1oz packet taco seasoning
1 tsp garlic powder
1 tsp all-purpose seasoning
2 tsp ground coriander

01 Tip all the dried beans and chickpeas into the cooking pot. Add the stock and stir well with a wooden spoon. Tip in 2 of the salsa jars and spread the salsa over the beans, without mixing it in.

02 Secure the pressure cooker lid and set the valve to sealing. Pressure cook for 45 minutes, followed by a quick pressure release.

03 After releasing the pressure, add the remaining salsa, as well as all the remaining ingredients. Stir well and serve.

Mix & Match Note the ratio of beans to vegetable stock. We used 2 cups of beans to 4 cups of liquid. The ratio of beans to liquid is double the volume. If you hate kidney beans, you could double up on one of the other beans.

PASTA & RICE

HOW TO PRESSURE COOK PASTA

When we bought our first electric pressure cooker, Dom, being a chef, was straight on it. He wanted to see what he could make in a pressure cooker that was faster and easier than traditional cooking. One of the first things he tried was pasta. But why would a chef prefer pasta in the pressure cooker? Because you can just leave it to it. You don't need to check on it at all. You can prepare the rest of your dinner whilst it is busy pressure cooking. As a family, we have followed this method for many types of pasta, from spaghetti to fusilli to macaroni and penne. Like with many grains in the pressure cooker, it's all about the perfect ratio of pasta to liquid, combined with the perfect cooking time.

TOP TIPS

Pantry Spring Clean I often find myself with lots of different varieties of dried pasta with just a little left of each. Pasta bows, spirali, macaroni and conchiglie all have the same cooking time in the pressure cooker, so why not have a clear out and make a mixed pasta dish?

No-drain Pasta This is often the name given to pasta cooked in the pressure cooker. This is because you add just enough liquid so that, after it is pressure cooked, it soaks up the liquid and you don't need to drain the pasta. We prefer to have a little bit of liquid left over, though, as it makes a great base for a sauce.

Measure the Ratio One way to measure that you've got the right ratio of pasta and liquid is to check the water level. If it's about 1cm/½in above the pasta, then it's correct.

Want Onions? What I often do is sauté an onion first with some olive oil, then deglaze the pot with vegetable stock (sometimes wine, too). You then have a base for a pasta bake. It also works perfectly with our spaghetti and meatballs from page 162.

Stock or Water? You can use water or stock when you make pasta. I much prefer to use vegetable stock, because it gives the pasta a better flavour. If you're using stock, you won't need to add as much salt.

Favourite Pasta We have pressure cooked many types of pasta but our favourites are spirali, fusilli, macaroni, farfalle and rigatoni.

Go al Dente If you prefer pasta with a bite to it, then I recommend a 0-minute pressure cook and a 12-minute natural pressure release.

Portion Size On page 158 we make pasta salad jars, but we only need a small quantity of pasta. Using the pressure cooker method, you can make as little as 125g/4½oz pasta with 360ml/12½fl oz/1½ cups water. Remember, though – you can't go below this quantity of pasta, or there won't be enough liquid in the pot to go to pressure.

5-minute Pasta Sauce After pressure cooking the pasta, you should have about **180ml/6fl oz/¾ cup liquid** left over. If not, adjust to this. No need to press sauté, as the pressure cooker will still be nice and hot. Add in **1 × 280g/10oz tub cream cheese** (we use Philadelphia Light), along with **55g/2oz/⅔ cup grated Parmesan** and **1 heaped tablespoon garlic mayonnaise**. Stir in some salt and pepper, **1 teaspoon garlic powder** and **1 tablespoon dried oregano**. Stir well for a couple of minutes and, as if by magic, you have a creamy sauce.

QUICK PASTA FOR ANY OCCASION

This is the master recipe. Use it for pasta salads, add cream and cheese for macaroni cheese, or add wine, cream and shellfish for a seafood pasta.

SERVES **4**
FUNCTIONS **PRESSURE COOK**
PREP **2 MINUTES**
PRESSURE COOK TIME **3 MINUTES**
TOTAL COOK TIME **3 MINUTES**
CALORIES **435**

500g/1lb 2oz mixed dried pasta (we used spirali, pasta bows, macaroni and conchiglie)
1.4l/47fl oz/6 cups stock or water

01 Tip the dried pasta into the cooking pot. Pour in the liquid, season generously with salt and pepper, and stir. If using water instead of stock, add an extra teaspoon of sea salt. Make sure that the level of the liquid is above the top of the pasta.

02 Secure the pressure cooker lid, set the valve to sealing and pressure cook for 3 minutes, or 0 minutes for al dente, followed by a 12-minute natural pressure release. (The NPR is important as otherwise the starch from the pasta will create a syrup that comes out with the steam when releasing pressure. The longer you complete a natural pressure release, the more starch is retained.)

03 After releasing the remaining pressure, stir and you have ready-to-use, just-cooked pasta. But, of course, I don't want to leave it there. Turn the page and check out Sofia's pasta salad jars, which is the perfect use for your just-cooked pasta.

SOFIA'S BLT PASTA SALAD JARS

A packed lunch for school, food to take to work, a meal for a long drive or just a salad that is prepared in the fridge and ready to grab for people like me who work from home. With the ingredients in mind to make a BLT-style pasta salad, I asked Sofia to design this recipe for me using the new jars she'd bought for her school lunches. We air fry the bacon, pressure cook the pasta, and add a creamy, flavoured mayonnaise to make this a dream come true for food on the go.

MAKES **4 JARS**
FUNCTIONS **AIR FRY**
PREP **10 MINUTES**
AIR FRY COOK TIME **10 MINUTES**
TOTAL COOK TIME **10 MINUTES**
CALORIES **522**

400g/14oz bacon
¼ × portion quick pasta for any occasion (see page 157 – we used macaroni)
170g/6oz cherry tomatoes
1 tbsp balsamic vinegar
1 tbsp dried basil
28g/1oz/⅓ cup grated Parmesan
¼ medium red onion
1 Little Gem lettuce

CREAMY SALAD DRESSING

4 heaped tbsp mayonnaise (we use Hellmann's Light)
1 tbsp lemon juice
1 tbsp extra virgin olive oil
4 tbsp semi-skimmed/2% fat milk
1 tbsp dried chives
½ tsp garlic powder
¼ tsp mustard powder

01 Chop the bacon into small pieces and air fry at 200°C/400°F for 10 minutes. Set aside.

02 Mix together the creamy salad dressing ingredients and divide the mixture between 4 × 468ml/1 pint Mason jars. (If making kids' lunches, opt for plastic jars.)

03 Add the pasta to the jars, followed by the bacon bits.

04 Slice the cherry tomatoes in half, then tip them into a bowl and drizzle with the balsamic vinegar. Season them well with salt and pepper, then mix in the dried basil. Add the tomatoes on top of the bacon.

05 Sprinkle the Parmesan over the tomatoes, then peel and thinly slice the onion and add this, too.

06 Finally, roughly chop the lettuce and add this to the jar as the last ingredient. Seal the jars and store in the fridge until later.

SALAD JAR TIPS & TRICKS

Sauce at the Bottom, Lettuce at the Top It's important to follow this rule, as it will help you avoid soggy lettuce, and it also makes the salad last longer. Also, if you plan to tip the salad out onto a plate, the lettuce ends up on the bottom of the dish, as with a regular salad.

Customisable Sofia's excitement as she made these salad jars had us talking about alternatives she could make for her school lunch, such as tuna mayonnaise or a prawn cocktail.

Salad on the Go If you're eating them on the go, don't forget to take a fork! Just give them a quick shake before eating and tuck in.

Wide-mouth Jars It's not until you get into using jars for meal prep that you realise the importance of having 'wide-mouth' jars. The phrase refers to the fact that the top of the jar is not super skinny, so you're able to get your ingredients inside without making a mess.

Glass or Plastic I notice many brands sell glass jars – these aren't something I would want to use for travelling, but they are perfect for lunches at home. You can use either.

KITCHEN CUPBOARD PASTA BAKE

We call this kitchen cupboard pasta bake because it uses up ingredients that were neglected at the back of our kitchen cupboard – some odds and ends of pasta and leftover holiday seasoning. What do you have in your cupboard?

SERVES **4**
FUNCTIONS **PRESSURE COOK, GRILL/BROIL**
PREP **6 MINUTES**
PRESSURE COOK TIME **3 MINUTES**
GRILL COOK TIME **4 MINUTES**
TOTAL COOK TIME **7 MINUTES**
CALORIES **1396**

- 500g/1lb 2oz mixed dried pasta (we used spirali, pasta bows, macaroni and conchiglie)
- 1.4l/47fl oz/6 cups liquid (stock or water)
- 3 large boneless, skinless chicken breasts
- 240g/8½oz/1½ cups frozen sweetcorn

RANCH MAYONNAISE
- 3 heaped tbsp dried ranch seasoning
- 6 heaped tbsp mayonnaise (we use Hellmann's Light)
- 3 tbsp extra virgin olive oil
- 1 tsp mustard powder

PASTA SAUCE
- 1 × 300g/10½oz tub crème fraîche
- 2 tsp garlic purée
- 2 heaped tbsp dried ranch seasoning
- 2 tsp Dijon mustard
- 1 tbsp dried oregano
- 170g/6oz/1½ cups grated mature/sharp Cheddar

GRILLED TOPPING
- 12g/½oz/¼ cup breadcrumbs (we use panko)
- 55g/2oz/⅔ cup grated Parmesan

01 Tip the dried pasta into the cooking pot. Pour in the stock or water, season generously with salt and pepper, and stir. (If using water instead of stock add an extra teaspoon of sea salt.) Make sure that the liquid level is above the top of the pasta.

02 Place all the ranch mayonnaise ingredients in a bowl and mix well. Add the chicken breasts, season with salt and pepper, and turn to coat the chicken. Place the chicken gently over the pasta and liquid in the cooking pot, and any ranch mayonnaise remaining in the bowl can be smothered over the top of the chicken.

03 Secure the pressure cooker lid, set the valve to sealing and pressure cook for 3 minutes, followed by a 10-minute natural pressure release.

04 After releasing the remaining pressure, use a fork to lift the chicken breasts out of the cooking pot and place them on a clean chopping board.

05 Stir the pasta in the pot, then add all the pasta sauce ingredients. Let the heat from pressure cooking turn them into a creamy sauce. (If you've left the multicooker too long and it is cold, then you can set it to a medium sauté.)

06 Chop the chicken breast into chunks and add it to the pasta and sauce, along with the sweetcorn. Give it a good stir and check the seasoning.

07 Sprinkle the breadcrumbs and Parmesan on top, and set the multicooker to grill/broil at 220°C/430°F or 4 minutes, until golden and the cheese has melted. Serve straight away.

Milner Family Favourite As a mum, this recipe is particularly great because all you need to do is stack ingredients into the multicooker and, as if by magic, you have a creamy chicken pasta that you know will keep the kids full. It also works well as a recipe to cook ahead and reheat for when you're busy. This is a great example of a customisable pasta bake. This is our ranch version, but you could swap ranch for shawarma spices, Cajun seasoning or even peri peri. You can also mix and match the pasta shapes, as well as switching up the cheese. We use this recipe to use up different pasta shapes that we have left over.

DATE NIGHT SPAGHETTI & MEATBALLS

When I think of spaghetti and meatballs, my mind always drifts to *The Lady and the Tramp*, one of my favourite Disney movies, and the iconic spaghetti scene. Aside from the nostalgia, it's one of those delicious one-pot meals that shouts out comfort food. We use frozen meatballs because they keep their shape better. Everything goes into the cooking pot and a few short minutes later, after a quick mix with a wooden spoon, you have spaghetti and meatballs.

....

SERVES **4**
FUNCTIONS **SAUTÉ, PRESSURE COOK**
PREP **6 MINUTES**
SAUTÉ COOK TIME **5 MINUTES**
PRESSURE COOK TIME **3 MINUTES**
TOTAL COOK TIME **8 MINUTES**
CALORIES **701 (BEEF), 613 (PORK)**

....

1 medium brown onion
1 tbsp extra virgin olive oil
960ml/34fl oz/4 cups beef stock
24 frozen beef or pork meatballs (not chicken or turkey, as they will be too lean and may burn)
225g/8oz dried spaghetti
2 × 500g/1lb 2oz pasta sauce jars
2 tsp garlic purée
1 tbsp dried oregano
1 tbsp dried mixed herbs/Italian seasoning
1 tbsp dried thyme
15g/½oz Parmesan, thinly sliced, for sprinkling

01 Peel and chop the onion into small chunks, then add it to the cooking pot with the olive oil. Set the multicooker to sauté and when you hear the sizzle, stir and sauté until your onion has softened.

02 Press cancel and deglaze the cooking pot with half the stock. Add the meatballs in a single layer over the onions and stock. Break the spaghetti in half and add the pasta, being careful to spread it out so that there aren't any clumps, to prevent the pasta from sticking together whilst cooking.

03 Pour in the remaining stock, then tip in the pasta sauce. Refill one of the pasta sauce jars with water, attach the lid and shake. Add this liquid too, and make sure the pasta sauce and liquid cover the spaghetti fully. If not, use the back of a wooden spoon to press the pasta down into the liquid.

04 Secure the pressure cooker lid, set the valve to sealing and pressure cook for 3 minutes, followed by a 10-minute natural pressure release.

05 After releasing the remaining pressure, add the garlic purée, all the herbs and a generous seasoning of salt and pepper. Give it a good stir. It will look like a soup when you first remove the lid but will thicken as you stir and as the pasta absorbs the liquid.

06 Divide between bowls and sprinkle over a little sliced Parmesan to serve.

GARLIC BREAD TOPPED LAZY LASAGNE

This is what to make when you fancy a lasagne but it feels like too much effort. The Bolognese ingredients slow cook with plenty of tomato sauce, then you just add strips of fresh lasagne, plenty of cheese and top with garlic bread.

....

SERVES **8**
FUNCTIONS **SAUTÉ, SLOW COOK, AIR FRY**
PREP **6 MINUTES**
SAUTÉ COOK TIME **5 MINUTES**
SLOW COOK TIME **4 HOURS**
AIR FRY COOK TIME **8 MINUTES**
TOTAL COOK TIME **4 HOURS 13 MINUTES**
CALORIES **623**

....

1 medium brown onion
1 tbsp extra virgin olive oil
675g/1½lb minced/ground beef
1.5kg/3lb 5oz/6 cups passata
2 tbsp tomato purée/paste
1 tbsp garlic powder
1 tbsp dried basil
2 heaped tbsp dried oregano
2 tbsp mixed herbs/Italian seasoning
225g/8oz/2 cups grated mature/ sharp Cheddar
500g/1lb 2oz/2 cups pasta sauce
1 × 250g/9oz pack fresh lasagne sheets
2 tbsp roughly chopped fresh basil
55g/2oz/⅔ cup grated Parmesan
1 fresh garlic bread baguette, sliced

01 Press sauté and, as it warms up, peel and dice the onion. Add the onion to the cooking pot with the olive oil and, when you hear the sizzle, sauté until the onion has softened. Add the beef and sauté until lightly brown.

02 Cancel sauté and stir in the passata, tomato purée, garlic powder and dried herbs. Season generously with salt and pepper. Secure the multicooker lid and slow cook for 3 hours on high.

03 Stir the pot and add the Cheddar and pasta sauce. Refill the pasta sauce jar with water, secure the lid and shake it, then pour it into the pot.

04 Using scissors, cut the lasagne sheets into 2cm/¾in strips. Stir these into the Bolognese and replace the lid. Slow cook for another hour.

05 Add half the fresh basil and give it a good stir. Sprinkle in half the Parmesan and cover the top with slices of garlic bread. Replace the lid and set the multicooker to air fry at 180°C/360°F for 8 minutes, or until the bread is crispy and the garlic butter has melted.

06 Serve with the remaining Parmesan and basil leaves sprinkled on top. We also like to serve ours with some salad leaves on the side, which have been drizzled with olive oil and sprinkled with Parmesan.

Mix & Match You can use any combination of pasta sauce, canned tomatoes and passata. Just remember a total weight of 2kg/4lb 8oz/8 cups liquid. Perfect for when you're clearing out the pantry!

Food Stretcher Make it stretch further by adding another jar of pasta sauce, refilling the empty jar with water and adding this, too. The lazy lasagne turns into a soup!

Must Try Lasagne Chips Move over tortilla chips – these taste even better. Use scissors to chop leftover fresh lasagne sheets into 2cm/¾in strips and place in a bowl with 1 tablespoon of extra virgin olive oil and 1 teaspoon each of dried oregano and dried thyme. Mix with your hands until evenly coated. Transfer to the air fryer basket/crisp plate and spread the chips out for an even cook. Air fry for 8 minutes at 180°C/360°F, or until crispy to your liking. We serve ours with ketchup.

HOW TO PRESSURE COOK RICE

Calling all rice fans! Your life will change forever once you use your multicooker to make a bowl of rice. It's just a case of working out the ratios of liquid to rice and cooking times, but once I have shown you how, there is no going back. I first made rice using the electric pressure cooker back in 2017 and have loved it since.

Simply add the rinsed rice to the cooking pot, pour in the liquid, secure the lid, set it to the correct cooking time, and when you come back to the multicooker, bingo, you have perfect rice. Just mix and match the herbs, spices, stock and water to create your own ideal rice.

COCONUT LIME JASMINE RICE

If I could only make one type of rice for the rest of my life it would be this. It tastes like a lot of effort has been put into making it, but it is very straightforward. The coconut milk makes it creamy whilst the coriander and the lime flavour it to perfection.

SERVES 2
FUNCTIONS PRESSURE COOK
PREP 4 MINUTES
PRESSURE COOK TIME 3 MINUTES
TOTAL COOK TIME 3 MINUTES
CALORIES 961

- 300g/10½oz/1½ cups jasmine rice
- 1 × 400g/14oz can coconut milk
- 2 tbsp frozen chopped garlic
- 2 tbsp frozen chopped coriander/cilantro
- 1 tbsp frozen chopped ginger
- 3 tbsp fresh lime juice
- 1 tbsp garlic purée
- 3 tbsp finely chopped fresh coriander/cilantro

01 Wash the jasmine rice in a mesh strainer under cold water, shaking it about, until the water runs clear.

02 Tip the rinsed rice into the cooking pot and pour in the coconut milk. Quarter-fill the can and give it a shake to remove any bits stuck to the sides, then pour this into the pot. Sprinkle in the frozen garlic, coriander and ginger, then give it a stir with a silicone spatula and make sure all the rice is covered in liquid.

03 Secure the pressure cooker lid, set the valve to sealing, and pressure cook for 3 minutes, followed by a 10-minute natural pressure release.

04 After releasing the remaining pressure, remove the lid and add the lime juice, garlic purée, chopped fresh coriander and a generous seasoning of salt and pepper. Stir the rice and fluff it up with a silicone spatula before serving.

RICE 101

My Rice Is Too Mushy Reduce the cooking time the next time you make it by a couple of minutes.

My Rice Still Has a Bite Increase the cooking time by a couple of minutes.

My Rice Is Too Sticky Add a tablespoon of olive oil to the rice before cooking, the next time you make it.

My Rice Sticks to the Bottom of the Cooking Pot Sauté an onion in some butter in the cooking pot before adding and cooking the rice. This will coat the bottom of the cooking pot and prevent sticking.

TOP TIPS

NPR Ten minutes probably seems like a long time to let the rice sit after its quick pressure cook, but this is because the multicooker acts like a steamer and is continuing to cook the rice slowly.

Wash It You will often see the word 'rinsed' associated with rice. This is when you wash rice in a mesh strainer under cold water until the water runs clear. What this does is remove any dirt and excess starch.

Oil It We recommend that you add a tablespoon of extra virgin olive oil to the rice in the strainer after rinsing it. Give it a shake and this little bit of oil will stop the rice clumping together as it cooks.

Pot It I love being able to cook multiple things at once in the cooking pot. Usually, you have to add a trivet to layer up the food. With rice, you can just add it first so it sits at the bottom or you can put it on top. The top method is perfect if you're cooking a curry below (see page 172).

Flavour It You can add your favourite dried herbs and spices, or sauces to the rice when you cook it. We love to make our rice with salsa, like on page 168.

Vegetable It You can add frozen chopped vegetables to the rice and it will all cook together. We buy the bags of mixed vegetables, but you could add sweetcorn, peas, diced carrots or onion individually.

Liquid It You have a few options when it comes to adding liquid to the rice, but you need it to go to pressure. For this reason, avoid using ingredients such as canned tomatoes. Instead, use water, flavoured stock, or watered down coconut milk (like we do in the recipe opposite).

Submerge It When you put the liquid over the rice, take a minute to stir the rice and make sure it is all beneath the surface of the liquid.

Best Rice We have tried many different types of rice in the multicooker but have found the best white rice is jasmine.

SALSA CHICKEN RICE BOX

Like the fast-food favourite, sliced chicken is served in a box over spicy rice. Our shortcut for the wow factor is using salsa instead of canned tomatoes in the rice. We then prepare the chicken in buttermilk for that creamy chicken. Because the chicken cooks over the rice, it makes it easy to cook in one pot and serve for lunch or dinner.

....

SERVES **4**
FUNCTIONS **SAUTÉ, PRESSURE COOK**
PREP **8 MINUTES**
MARINATING TIME **2 HOURS**
SAUTÉ COOK TIME **5 MINUTES**
PRESSURE COOK TIME **3 MINUTES**
TOTAL COOK TIME **8 MINUTES**
CALORIES **532**

....

240ml/8½fl oz/1 cup buttermilk
2 tbsp heaped southern fried chicken seasoning
4 medium boneless, skinless chicken breasts
1 red chilli, sliced, to serve (optional)
1 spring/green onion, sliced, to serve (optional)

SALSA RICE

½ medium red onion
½ red (bell) pepper/capsicum
1 tbsp extra virgin olive oil
1 tbsp garlic purée
1 × 300g/10½oz jar salsa dip
300g/10½oz/1½ cups jasmine rice, rinsed

01 Place the buttermilk and southern fried chicken seasoning in a shallow bowl. Give it a good mix with a dessertspoon. Add the chicken and turn the breasts to coat in the seasoned buttermilk. Cover with cling film/plastic wrap and marinate in the fridge for at least 2 hours, although overnight is best.

02 To make the salsa rice, set the multicooker to sauté. Peel and finely chop the onion, and deseed and finely chop the red pepper. Add them to the cooking pot with the olive oil. When you hear the sizzle, sauté until the onion has softened. Press cancel and stir in the garlic purée.

03 In a jug, create a salsa stock by combining 480ml/17fl oz/2 cups of water with 2 heaped tablespoons of the salsa. Pour this into the cooking pot to deglaze it, and scrape the bottom of the pot with a silicone spatula to remove any bits stuck on.

04 Tip the rinsed jasmine rice into the cooking pot, give it a stir and make sure the liquid covers it completely. Season generously with salt and pepper, then add 3 tablespoons of the salsa from the jar on to the rice. Using the back of a wooden spoon or spatula, spread the salsa out over the top of the rice, then place the marinated chicken breasts on top of this.

05 Secure the pressure cooker lid, set the valve to sealing, and pressure cook for 3 minutes, followed by a 10-minute natural pressure release

06 After releasing the remaining pressure, take the chicken out of the pot and place it on a clean chopping board to rest.

07 Add the remaining salsa to the rice (reserving a few teaspoons to serve), then give it another generous seasoning of salt and pepper, and stir and fluff up the rice with a silicone spatula.

08 Transfer the rice into bowls, slice the chicken breasts and serve the chicken over the rice, with any reseved salsa, and some sliced chilli and spring onion, if using.

Cooking One Without the Other The rice and the chicken both have the same cooking time. You could just make the rice or just the chicken, without the other. If making the chicken on its own, pour 360ml/12½fl oz/1½ cups of stock in the pot and add the air fryer basket/trivet for the chicken.

Extra Spice Prefer more of a spice kick? Add crushed dried chilli flakes to either the chicken marinade or the salsa rice: ¼ tsp – low/medium heat; ½ tsp – medium heat; 1 tsp – spicy.

HOW TO COOK 'POT IN POT' RICE

Also known as PIP, the idea is that you cook your rice in a container inside the cooking pot, rather than directly in the pot – so in pot . . . in . . . pot.

Why Not Throw It Straight in the Cooking Pot? You use PIP when you want to cook two things separately at the same time. You can cook a creamy curry in the main cooking pot, add a trivet, then put the little pot with rice on top. You could do the same with some chicken breasts and rice, or if you're making a chilli and fancy serving it with some rice. The possibilities are endless.

Why Not Put the Rice in First & the Meat Up Top? You can do this, too, and that's what we do on page 175 with our salmon and rice. I tend to do the rice at the bottom if there is more rice than protein in the finished dish. With a curry, the curry part of the dish is likely to be bigger than the rice, so I do PIP.

'POT IN POT' WHITE RICE

This is your master PIP rice recipe. I've used jasmine rice simply because it's the best rice for pressure cooking. Once you've made this as a practice run, you can mix and match the recipe with your favourite dried seasonings, or why not turn the page and make curry and rice?

SERVES **4**
FUNCTIONS **PRESSURE COOK**
PREP **2 MINUTES**
PRESSURE COOK TIME **6 MINUTES**
TOTAL COOK TIME **6 MINUTES**
CALORIES **272**

300g/10½oz/1½ cups jasmine rice, rinsed (see page 167)
360ml/12½fl oz/1½ cups vegetable stock

01 Pour 360ml/12½fl oz/1½ cups cold water into the cooking pot and add the trivet. The tall trivets or racks in the top position work best with PIP recipes.

02 Tip the jasmine rice into an 20cm/8in round silicone or stainless-steel container. Pour the stock into the container and stir with a silicone spatula, making sure all the rice is covered in the liquid. Lower the container onto your trivet.

03 Secure the pressure cooker lid, set the valve to sealing, and pressure cook for 6 minutes, followed by a full natural pressure release (about 7 minutes).

04 Carefully remove the hot container from the pressure cooker. Fluff up the rice, season with salt and pepper, and serve.

VEGETABLE RICE

When I see vegetable rice, it reminds me of eating out in Portugal. It is so easy to adapt your master rice recipe to make it. Simply add 210g/7½oz/1½ cups frozen diced vegetables with the rinsed rice and vegetable stock. I use the mixed bags of finely chopped carrots and green beans, along with sweetcorn and peas. At the end of the cooking time, season with salt, pepper and a tablespoon of dried thyme and you have vegetable rice.

HOW TO TURN 'POT IN POT' RICE INTO A MEAL

On page 172, we cook the butter chicken in the main cooking pot, add a trivet and a tin container, and the rice cooks up top. Use this method with other pressure-cooked meals with a similar cooking time, if you want to serve them with rice.

RICE COOKING TIMES

Sushi 1 cup rice, 1 cup liquid, 6 mins, 10npr

Arborio 1 cup rice, 3 cups liquid, 6 mins, 10npr

Basmati white rice 1 cup rice, 1½ cups liquid, 3 mins, 10npr

Long grain white rice 1 cup rice, 1½ cups liquid, 3 mins, 10npr

Basmati brown rice 1 cup rice, 1½ cups liquid, 10 mins, 10npr

Long grain brown rice 1 cup rice, 1¼ cups liquid, 18 mins, 5npr

OTHER GRAINS

Orzo 1 cup orzo, 1½ cups liquid, 3 mins, 10npr

Quinoa 1 cup quinoa, 1¼ cups liquid, 1 min, 12npr

CREAMY BUTTER CHICKEN & YELLOW RICE

Perfect for your next Indian fakeaway.

SERVES **4**
FUNCTIONS **SAUTÉ, PRESSURE COOK**
PREP **12 MINUTES**
SAUTÉ COOK TIME **5 MINUTES**
PRESSURE COOK TIME **3 MINUTES**
TOTAL COOK TIME **8 MINUTES**
CALORIES **838**

1 large brown onion
55g/2oz/¼ cup salted butter or ghee
1 tbsp cumin seeds
2 tbsp garam masala
1 tbsp ground coriander
1 tbsp tomato purée/paste
2 tbsp medium curry powder
480ml/17fl oz/2 cups chicken stock
500g/1lb 2oz/2 cups passata
1 × 400g/14oz can chopped tomatoes
1 medium cauliflower
4 large boneless, skinless chicken breasts
2 tsp each ginger and garlic purée
4 tbsp double/heavy/thickened cream
2 tbsp chopped fresh coriander/cilantro

YELLOW RICE
200g/7oz/1 cup jasmine rice, rinsed
240ml/8½fl oz/1 cup vegetable stock
½ tsp chopped fresh coriander/cilantro
½ tsp turmeric

SOFIA'S CURRY PASTE
1 garlic bulb, cloves peeled
28g/1oz root ginger, peeled
2 tsp ground coriander
1 tbsp chopped fresh coriander/cilantro
1 tsp cumin seeds
2 tsp garam masala
2 tsp turmeric
½ tsp chilli powder
3 tbsp tomato purée/paste
1 small brown onion, peeled

01 Place all the curry paste ingredients in a small food processor or blender, or use a pestle and mortar, and blitz until it becomes a smooth paste. (Sofia has her own mini food processor that she uses for this.) Set aside for adding later.

02 Peel and thinly slice the large brown onion and place it in the cooking pot with the butter or ghee. Press sauté and, when you hear the sizzle, sauté the onion until softened. Press cancel, and add the cumin seeds, garam masala, ground coriander, tomato purée and half the curry powder.

03 Stir in the stock, passata and canned tomatoes, then break the cauliflower into florets and add them to the pot.

04 Spread half the curry paste over the chicken breasts, then place them on top of the veg in the pot, without stirring them into the sauce. Season them with salt, pepper and the remaining curry powder.

05 To make the yellow rice, place the rice in a 20cm/8in cake tin/pan. Pour in the stock, along with the coriander and turmeric, and stir. Wrap the top of the tin tightly in foil. Place a tall trivet or rack in the top position over the chicken, and move it about until it feels sturdy. Lower the cake tin of rice onto the trivet or rack.

06 Secure the pressure cooker lid, set the valve to sealing, and pressure cook for 3 minutes, followed by a 6-minute natural pressure release.

07 After releasing the pressure, remove the rice tin, then the trivet, and finally remove the chicken and place it on a clean chopping board.

08 Use a fork to fluff up the rice. Use a wooden spoon to break up some of the bigger bits of cauliflower and stir the remaining curry paste into the cooking pot, along with the ginger and the garlic purées. Chop the chicken into bite-sized pieces, then add them back into the cooking pot. Stir in the cream, most of the chopped fresh coriander, and season generously with salt and pepper.

09 Serve the butter chicken with the rice, and sprinkle with the reserved coriander.

Naan Bread Curry When I worked at an Indian takeaway in my teens, they always had lots of curry left over. The next day they would serve the curry over naan bread and it was always a huge hit. Spread a dessertspoon of the curry sauce over the top of the naan, then add some thinly sliced chicken on top. Finish with a sprinkling of fresh coriander/cilantro. Place it in the air fryer basket/crisp plate and air fry at 180°C/360°F for 4 minutes before serving.

MARINATED SALMON & VEGETABLE RICE

Let's go back to front. Well back to front in the world of PIP pressure cooking, at least. With the butter chicken and rice on page 172, we cooked the chicken at the bottom and the rice up top. This is the other way around - vegetable rice at the bottom and marinated salmon in the tin/pan up top.

....

SERVES **2**
FUNCTIONS **SAUTÉ, PRESSURE COOK**
PREP **10 MINUTES**
MARINATING TIME **2 HOURS**
SAUTÉ COOK TIME **5 MINUTES**
PRESSURE COOK TIME **3 MINUTES**
TOTAL COOK TIME **8 MINUTES**
CALORIES **584**

....

4 × 115g/4oz salmon fillets

MARINADE
120g/4¼oz oyster sauce
3 tbsp sweet chilli sauce
120ml/4fl oz/½ cup clear honey
1 tbsp light soy sauce
1 tbsp fresh lime juice
2 tsp garlic purée
2 tsp ginger purée

VEGETABLE RICE
210g/7½oz/1½ cups frozen mixed vegetables (we use carrots, peas and broccoli)
1 tbsp extra virgin olive oil
360ml/12½fl oz/1½ cups vegetable stock
200g/7oz/1 cup jasmine rice, rinsed
2 tsp Chinese five spice

01 Start by marinating the salmon. Add the marinade ingredients to a bowl, mix well with a dessertspoon, then add the salmon fillets. Season with salt and pepper, and turn to coat the fillets in the marinade. Cover the bowl with cling film/plastic wrap and marinate in the fridge for at least 2 hours, although overnight is best.

02 Press sauté on the multicooker, add the frozen veg and the olive oil, and warm through to defrost the vegetables and create an oily coating to the bottom of the cooking pot. This will help the rice cook better. Press cancel and deglaze the pot with the stock.

03 Add the rinsed rice and Chinese five spice, and stir, making sure all the rice is covered by the stock (otherwise there will be some hard bits of rice). Place the tall trivet or rack in the top position over the rice. Arrange the marinated salmon in a foil tray (you don't need to use a tray but we find it helps to keep the flavours in the salmon), then place the tray on the trivet or rack.

04 Secure the pressure cooker lid, set the valve to sealing, and pressure cook for 3 minutes, followed by a 10-minute natural pressure release.

05 After releasing the remaining pressure, remove the foil tray and the trivet or rack. Drizzle a couple of tablespoons of the marinade from the tray into the rice, then stir and fluff up the rice. Season the salmon and the rice with salt and pepper, then serve together with the leftover marinade.

KYLE'S BUTTERNUT SQUASH RISOTTO

This is an easy risotto that will remind you of a Mediterranean restaurant. It is seriously addictive but, when you read the recipe, you'll be wondering how something can taste so good, when it has such simple, everyday ingredients. Inspired by a dish I ate on holiday, you can have an Italian night at home on a budget with this delicious recipe.

....

SERVES **4**
FUNCTIONS **SAUTÉ, PRESSURE COOK**
PREP **10 MINUTES**
SAUTÉ COOK TIME **5 MINUTES**
PRESSURE COOK TIME **6 MINUTES**
TOTAL COOK TIME **11 MINUTES**
CALORIES **344**

....

1 medium brown onion
2 tbsp salted butter (straight from the fridge)
2 tbsp frozen chopped garlic
120ml/4fl oz/½ cup dry white wine
960ml/34fl oz/4 cups vegetable stock
2 pinches saffron strands
2 tsp turmeric
1 tbsp smoked paprika
2–3 tsp dried thyme
220g/8oz/1½ cups arborio rice, rinsed
200g/7oz butternut squash, peeled and diced into 2cm/¾in cubes (prepared weight)
1 tbsp finely chopped fresh thyme
1 tbsp grated Parmesan

01 Peel and finely chop the onion. Add the butter to the cooking pot, cutting it into cubes as you do, then tip in the onion and press sauté. As it warms up and the butter melts, stir the onion with a wooden spoon. Continue to sauté until the butter has melted and the onion has softened (taking care that the butter doesn't burn).

02 Press cancel and stir in the frozen garlic. Deglaze the pot with the white wine and the stock, then stir in all the spices and herbs.

03 Add the rice, stirring to make sure it is fully submerged, then place the butternut squash on top of the liquid, without stirring again.

04 Secure the pressure cooker lid, set the valve to sealing and pressure cook for 6 minutes, followed by a 10-minute natural pressure release.

05 After releasing the remaining pressure, give the risotto a good stir and add a generous seasoning of salt and pepper. Sprinkle over the thyme and Parmesan to serve.

You Only Need a Little Squash The amount of squash many seem small, but when the meal comes together it's just the right quantity. If you're buying a large squash, why not prepare the whole thing and air fry some for another day? Air fry for 15 minutes at 180°C/360°F – it's even better with a sprinkling of roughly chopped basil.

Risotto First Timer I know many people have not made a risotto before, and it can be nerve wracking for a first timer. I set Kyle the challenge of making this recipe. He proudly told us that he didn't burn it and he has made it several times since, and it is now his favourite recipe from the book!

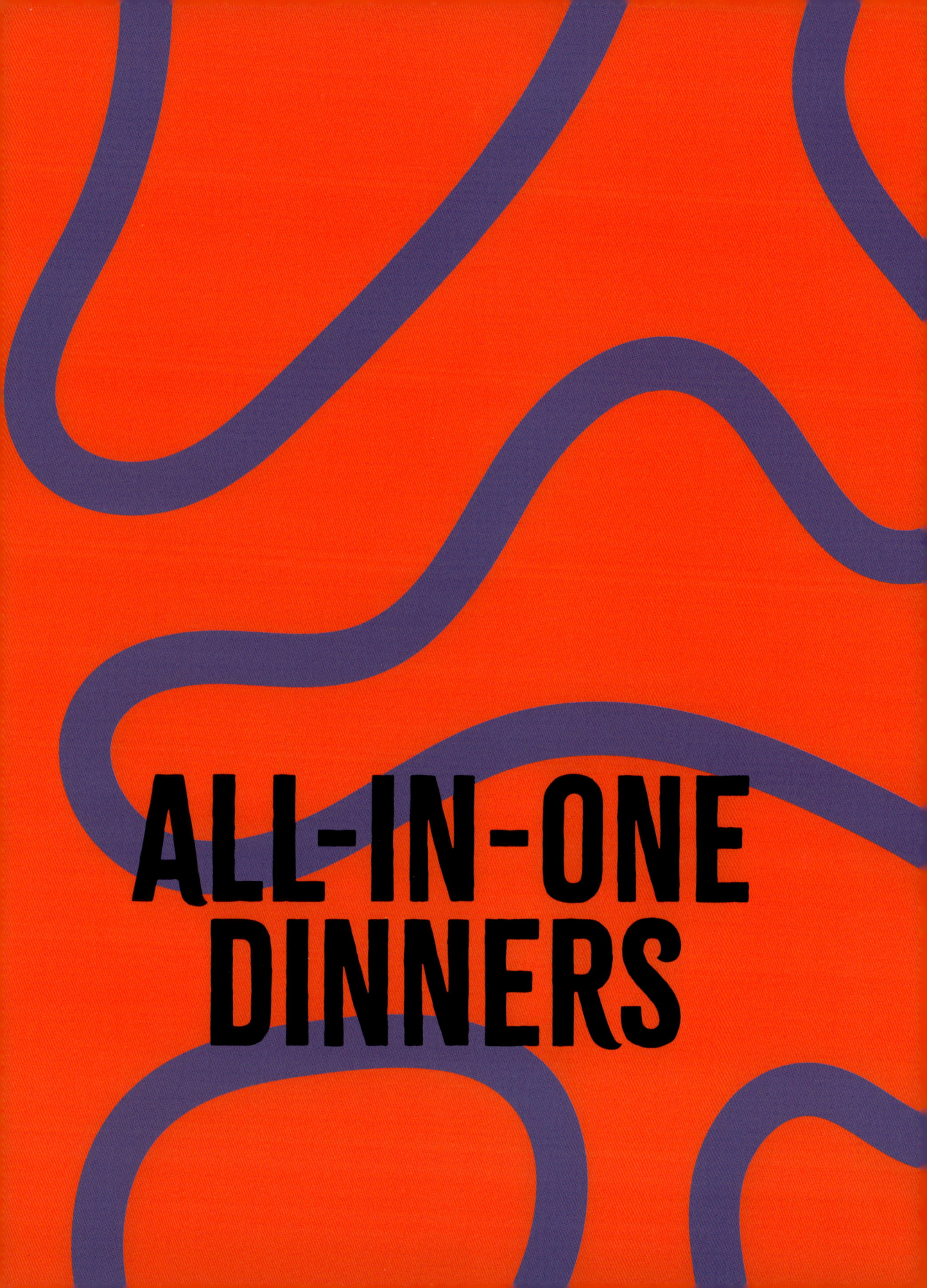

HOW TO MAKE ALL-IN-ONE STEAM MEALS

Our newest multicooker has a steam meals option and our other machine has a speedi meals option. In this chapter, we show you how to use these settings to stack meals. Using the two-tier rack, you can cook your protein, veg and carbs all at the same time. Steam meals are often called rapid meals, simply because, on average, a full meal will take just 10 minutes to cook. You could also cook using just two layers of food (check out our Caribbean bowls with a layer of vegetables and rice on page 188). We start the chapter with steak noodle bowls as they're an easy introduction to steam meals – it's just noodles, broth, pak choi and steak!

No Steam Meals Setting? Not all multicookers are equal and if you don't have this setting, go back to the recipes in the pasta and rice chapter (see pages 156–177) that teach you how to cook ingredients over pasta and rice using the pressure cook setting.

Steam Meals Cooking Time After lots of experiments with steam meals, we have found the average is 10 minutes at 180°C/360°F. Use this as your guide when trying to understand the time and temperature. This chapter will also help you get started.

VIETNAMESE-STYLE STEAK NOODLE BOWLS

SERVES **2**
FUNCTIONS **SAUTÉ, STEAM MEALS**
PREP **8 MINUTES**
MARINATING TIME **2 HOURS**
SAUTÉ COOK TIME **3 MINUTES**
STEAM MEALS COOK TIME **5 MINUTES**
TOTAL COOK TIME **8 MINUTES**
CALORIES **910**

- 2 × 225g/8oz ribeye steaks
- 1 medium brown onion
- 1 tbsp extra virgin olive oil
- 90g/3¼oz quick-cook noodles
- 960ml/34fl oz/4 cups beef bone broth
- 1 pak choi/bok choy
- 1 tbsp nasi goreng paste
- 1 spring/green onion

MARINADE
- 3 tbsp extra virgin olive oil
- 2 tbsp ginger purée
- 2 tbsp fish sauce
- 2 tsp lemongrass paste
- 1 tbsp frozen chopped garlic
- 55g/2oz/¼ cup soft brown sugar

01 Add all the marinade ingredients to a bowl, and mix well. Place the steaks in a shallow bowl and drizzle over 2 tablespoons of the marinade. Turn the steaks in the marinade to make sure they get a good coating, then leave to marinate in the fridge for 2 hours.

02 Finely chop the brown onion and place in the cooking pot with the olive oil. Press sauté and wait for the sizzle. Sauté the onion for a few minutes, then press cancel.

03 Add the noodles to the pot and pour over the broth. (Make sure you pour the broth over the noodles, as this will prevent any of them getting dry.)

04 Place the 2-tier rack into the cooking pot over the noodles. Add a layer of foil to the bottom tier, then clean and shred the pak choi, and arrange the pak choi on the foil tier. Cover the top tier with foil, then place the marinated steaks on top. (I always use foil in order to catch the marinade.) Drizzle any marinade left on the plate over the steak.

05 Secure the lid on the multicooker, press steam meals and set the temperature to 180°C/360°F and a cooking time of 5 minutes. The pot will warm up before it starts counting down, very much like a steamer does.

06 When the multicooker beeps, remove the 2-tier rack and stir the noodles. Add the remaining marinade to the noodles, then stir in the pak choi. Remove the steaks and slice them into strips, then add these, too. Finish by stirring in the nasi goreng paste and a generous seasoning of salt and pepper. Serve in bowls with thinly sliced spring onion sprinkled on top.

CHICKEN KATSU CURRY WITH SUSHI RICE

I love katsu curry and, in this recipe, we make a curry sauce that can be served cold as a mayonnaise, for taking your katsu to work, or warm as a curry with rice. As this uses the tiered system, it's very easy to get the recipe quickly on the go for a midweek dinner.

SERVES **2**
FUNCTIONS **STEAM MEALS, AIR FRY**
PREP **15 MINUTES**
MARINATING TIME **1 HOUR**
STEAM MEALS COOK TIME **10 MINUTES**
AIR FRY COOK TIME **3 MINUTES**
TOTAL COOK TIME **13 MINUTES**
CALORIES **1204**

2 medium chicken breasts
40g/1½oz/¾ cup panko breadcrumbs
225g/8oz/1 cup sushi rice, rinsed
480ml/16½fl oz/2 cups chicken stock
170g/6oz sugar snap peas
¼ tsp Chinese five spice
Extra virgin olive oil spray

KATSU SAUCE
240ml/8½fl oz/1 cup coconut cream
2 heaped tbsp katsu curry paste
2 tsp garlic purée
½ tsp ground ginger
1 tsp garam masala
½ tsp turmeric

01 Add all the katsu sauce ingredients to a bowl and mix with a spoon. Place half the mixture in a shallow bowl, then add the chicken breasts and season well with salt and pepper. Turn to coat the chicken breasts thoroughly in the sauce, then cover the bowl in cling film/plastic wrap and leave the chicken to marinate in the fridge for 1 hour, or overnight if you have the time. Place the remaining katsu sauce in the fridge as well, until you are ready to use it.

02 After marinating, the chicken is ready to be breaded. Tip the breadcrumbs into a separate shallow bowl. One at a time, place the chicken breasts in the breadcrumbs and turn to coat completely.

03 Next, add the rice to the bottom of the cooking pot, then pour in the stock and mix well, making sure all the rice is covered by the stock. Place a layer of foil on the bottom tier of the 2-tier rack. Arrange the sugar snap peas on the foil-covered tier. Sprinkle the peas with the Chinese five spice and give it a little spray of olive oil. Add the top tier and click it into place. Place the 2-tier rack with the peas in the cooking pot and make sure it's sturdy. Now place the breaded chicken on the top tier, spreading it out so that you can achieve a golden crisp on your chicken.

04 Secure the lid of the multicooker, press steam meals and set the temperature to 180°C/360°F and a cooking time of 10 minutes. The pot will warm up before it starts counting down, very much like a steamer does.

05 When the multicooker beeps, check the internal temperature of the chicken. It needs to reach 70°C/160°F or above. To serve warm curry sauce with the chicken, and not a katsu mayonnaise, remove the chicken, rice and peas, and place a ramekin of the sauce on the rack and air fry for 3 minutes at 180°C/360°F.

06 Serve the breaded chicken with the sauce, peas and sushi rice.

10-MINUTE MOROCCAN-SPICED LAMB STEAKS

With this lamb recipe, we cook a casserole in the bottom of the pot and lamb steaks with a Moroccan crust up top.

SERVES **4**
FUNCTIONS **STEAM MEALS**
PREP **15 MINUTES**
STEAM MEALS COOK TIME **10 MINUTES**
TOTAL COOK TIME **10 MINUTES**
CALORIES **685**

1 large sweet potato
½ red (bell) pepper/capsicum
240g/8½oz cauliflower
1 × 400g/14oz can chopped tomatoes
1 × 400g/14oz can chickpeas, drained
1 tbsp harissa paste
1 tbsp garlic purée
2–3 tsp ground cinnamon
2 tsp mixed spice/apple spice
2 tsp ground cumin
2 × 225g/8oz lamb steaks
500g/1lb 2 oz/2 cups passata
1 tbsp chopped fresh coriander/cilantro

LAMB CRUST
2 tsp ground coriander
2 tsp smoked paprika
2 tsp harissa paste
3 tbsp extra virgin olive oil

TO ADD LATER
1 tbsp smoked paprika
1 tbsp ground cumin
1 tbsp harissa paste

01 Peel and chop the sweet potatoes into 1cm/½in cubes. Deseed and chop the pepper into pieces a similar size. Break the cauliflower into small florets. Add the veg to the cooking pot, along with the tomatoes, chickpeas, harissa paste, garlic and all the herbs and spices (except the Lamb Crust and To Add Later spices). Give it a good stir.

02 Set the rack in place, then cover it with a layer of foil. Place the lamb steaks on top and season them well with salt and pepper. Mix the lamb crust ingredients together in a small bowl, then use a pastry brush to coat the lamb steaks in an even layer of the crust.

03 Secure the lid on the multicooker, press steam meals and set the temperature to 180°C/360°F and a cooking time of 10 minutes. The pot will warm up before it starts counting down, very much like a steamer does.

04 When the multicooker beeps, remove the rack with the lamb and set it aside to rest. Stir the veg in the cooking pot and sprinkle in the To Add Later seasonings. Use a stick blender to blitz a small amount of the casserole, then stir this in, to thicken the sauce. Finally, stir in the passata.

05 Slice the steaks into strips and serve the lamb on a bed of the veggie casserole with roughly chopped coriander sprinkled on top.

Prefer a Stew? If you'd rather a less thick sauce, add the can of chopped tomatoes to the pot, then refill the can with water, give it a shake, and add that, too. The sauce will be just as delicious but will be more of a stew.

MAPLE GINGER SALMON PACKETS

When we were in Florida, room service was our go-to in the evenings after a day of theme park rides with tired kids. There were about 15 different meals to choose from, but my favourite was the delicious ginger salmon with steamed rice and broccolini. Using that room service dinner as inspiration, I have transformed salmon, rice and broccolini into an easy steam meal.

SERVES **2**
FUNCTIONS **STEAM MEALS**
PREP **8 MINUTES**
MARINATING TIME **1 HOUR**
STEAM MEALS COOK TIME **10 MINUTES**
TOTAL COOK TIME **10 MINUTES**
CALORIES **957**

- 2 × 115g/4oz salmon fillets
- 210g/7½oz/1 cup basmati white rice, rinsed
- 1½ tsp extra virgin olive oil
- 480ml/17fl oz/2 cups vegetable stock
- 170g/6oz broccolini
- 1 tsp salted butter

MARINADE
- 2 tbsp soy sauce
- 1 tsp oyster sauce
- 2 tbsp maple syrup
- 2 tsp garlic purée
- 2 tsp ginger purée
- 2 tsp finely chopped fresh coriander/cilantro
- 1 red chilli, deseeded and finely chopped, plus extra to serve
- 2 spring/green onions, finely chopped, plus extra to serve

01 Mix the marinade ingredients together in a bowl, add the salmon fillets and turn to coat them well. Leave the salmon to marinate in the fridge for at least 1 hour, or overnight, if possible, for the best flavour.

02 Add the rice to the cooking pot, then add the olive oil and mix well. (This will stop the basmati sticking when it cooks.) Pour in the stock and stir.

03 Get out the 2-tier rack and add a layer of foil to the bottom tier. Arrange the broccolini on the foiled tier and season it well with salt and pepper. Dot the butter on top, so that it can melt onto the veg as it cooks. Place the 2-tier rack in the cooking pot over the rice.

04 Create a foil packet by placing one big strip of foil on top of another strip in the shape of a cross. Place the salmon in the centre, then fold the sides of the foil up to create a packet, leaving a small gap at the top. (This helps the salmon cook more quickly. You don't want it to be tightly sealed.) Position the salmon packet on the top tier.

05 Secure the multicooker lid and set to steam meals at 180°C/360°F for 10 minutes.

06 When the multicooker beeps, remove the 2-tier rack. Stir the rice, then divide it between 2 plates. Serve the rice with the salmon, any cooking juices from the foil packet, a sprinkle of chilli and spring onion, and the broccolini.

CARIBBEAN SUMMER VEG WITH RICE & PEAS

I love the Caribbean classic rice and peas. I also love Caribbean summer vegetables and, yes, that includes pineapple. With the rice cooking at the bottom of the cooking pot, and a big foil layer of pineapple, courgette, red onion and red pepper at the top – they become a 'bowl in one'!

....

SERVES **4**
FUNCTIONS **SAUTÉ, STEAM MEALS**
PREP **8 MINUTES**
SAUTÉ COOK TIME **8 MINUTES**
STEAM MEALS COOK TIME **10 MINUTES**
TOTAL COOK TIME **18 MINUTES**
CALORIES **751**

....

1 yellow or green courgette/zucchini
1 small red onion
1 red (bell) pepper/capsicum
1 scotch bonnet (adjust for your heat level)
225g/8oz fresh pineapple chunks
2 tsp ground allspice
2–3 tsp dried thyme
55g/2oz/¼ cup salted butter
285g/10oz/1 cup jerk barbecue sauce

COCONUT RICE

300g/10½oz/1½ cups jasmine rice, rinsed
1 × 400g/14oz can coconut milk
2 tbsp frozen chopped garlic
2 tbsp frozen chopped coriander/cilantro
1 tbsp frozen chopped ginger
100g/3½oz/½ cup cooked kidney beans (see recipe note right)
2 tsp ground allspice
2 tsp finely chopped fresh coriander/cilantro

01 Trim and chop the courgette into 1cm/½in chunks. Peel and chop the onion. Deseed and chop the pepper. Deseed and finely chop the scotch bonnet. Add all these vegetables to the cooking pot, along with the pineapple, allspice, thyme and butter. Press sauté and wait for the sizzle. Sauté the veg as the butter melts. (We do this to flavour the cooking pot before making the steam meal.) After about an 8-minute sauté, remove the veg and place them in a bowl for later. Add the jerk barbecue sauce to the bowl with the veg and stir well.

02 Place the rice in the cooking pot and pour in the coconut milk. Quarter-fill the empty can with water, shake it about, then pour this into the pot, too. Add the garlic, coriander and ginger, and mix well.

03 Place the rack over the rice and cover it in foil. Carefully place the barbecue vegetables on the foil-covered rack, creating a space at each side so that you can easily add them and take them out of the rack without the food flying off.

04 Secure the lid on the multicooker, press steam meals and cook for 10 minutes at 180°C/360°F.

05 Remove the vegetables from the cooking pot, along with the rack, and set aside. Add the kidney beans, allspice, chopped fresh coriander and a generous seasoning of salt and pepper to the rice, and stir well.

06 Divide the rice and peas between 4 bowls and serve with the veg spooned on top.

Cooking Kidney Beans Using the Pressure Cooker We always cook our own dried kidney beans using the pressure cooker button of the multicooker. Add 190g/6½oz/1 cup dried kidney beans and 300ml/10fl oz/1¼ cups water, then pressure cook for 40 minutes, and you have kidney beans ready for this recipe without soaking a single bean. You can read more about our no-soak beans on page 17.

Not Had Rice & Peas Before? This is a delicious Jamaican combo of white rice and red kidney beans. If you've not had it before, it may surprise you to know that the 'peas' in the recipe are actually beans. Just in case you're skimming the recipe and looking for peas! I do think 'rice and peas' has more of a ring to it than 'rice and beans'!

HOW TO PROVE BREAD

There is something special about the smell of homemade bread, and better than that even is eating the fresh loaf you've just made. But the task of proving bread when you have a busy lifestyle seems such an effort… that is until you try the prove setting on your multicooker followed by steam bread! I challenged Dom to not only make a loaf using the prove setting, but also to transform the same dough into beer bread and focaccia. I got the lucky job of sitting in our kitchen watching him slice that first loaf. It was incredible, not just how good the bread tasted but, thanks to the prove setting, how fast it was to make.

DOM'S BREAD DOUGH FOR EVERYTHING

This dough is incredibly versatile. Beyond the classic loaf and focaccia, you can also use it for bread rolls. Just use a good silicone loaf tin/pan or tray.

SERVES **6-8**
FUNCTIONS **PROVE**
PREP **15 MINUTES**
PROVE TIME **60 MINUTES**
TOTAL COOK TIME **60 MINUTES**
CALORIES **155-116**

260g/9½oz/1¾ cups plain/all-purpose flour
1½ tsp instant yeast
1 tsp salt
180ml/6fl oz/¾ cup warm water

01 Add the flour, yeast and salt to a bowl.

02 Gradually pour in the warm water, a little at a time, and mix with your hands until you have a dough.

03 Knead the dough on a lightly floured work surface for about 10 minutes until lovely and smooth.

04 Transfer the dough to a greased silicone loaf tin/pan (for a loaf) or a square silicone tin (for focaccia). Place the pan onto the air fryer basket/crisp plate in the cooking pot. Press prove on the multicooker/air fryer, set the temperature to 35°C/95°F, and prove for 60 minutes.

05 When the multicooker beeps, to your amazement your dough will have proved and doubled in size. It's ready to bake.

Proving Bread Temperatures Depending on the brand of your multicooker, the proving temperature can vary. We have found the sweet spot is 35°C/95°F. In the first air fryer we owned with a prove setting, the standard was 75°C/170°F. It did an OK job, but it was partly cooking the bread while it proved, which often resulted in the bread being dry.

The Size of Your Multicooker Multicookers come in all shapes and sizes. You have round ones, like a slow cooker or pressure cooker, whilst others are an extension of the air fryer. We have demonstrated with our FlexDrawer, which we use a lot for dehydrating, proving and air frying. If you are using a different shape to ours, you can adjust the size of the dough.

Bread Versus Air Fry I had the wonderful job of comparing Dom's steam bread with his air fry bread. Steam won the race easily and looked golden. Air fry was paler but still tasted nice. If you have the steam bread option, use it.

Grease the Silicone Even though we use silicone loaf pans for our bread, we do notice it still sticks a fair bit. So, even though it's silicone, spray it with a little olive oil and rub it all over.

WEEKNIGHT BEER BREAD

Beer bread is our favourite bread. It's a very simple concept – you swap the warm water from a typical bread dough for any wheat beer. It makes a very flavoursome bread, without it being overpowering, and you can also add some cheese. If I was to choose a starting point for making your first loaf of bread in the multicooker, it would be this.

....

SERVES **8**
FUNCTIONS **PROVE, STEAM BREAD/AIR FRY**
PREP **15 MINUTES**
PROVE TIME **60 MINUTES**
STEAM BAKE/AIR FRY COOK TIME **20 MINUTES**
TOTAL COOK TIME **80 MINUTES**
CALORIES **122**

....

260g/9½oz/1¾ cups plain/all-purpose flour
1½ tsp instant yeast
1 tsp salt
180ml/6fl oz/¾ cup wheat beer, room temperature (we use Erdinger)

01 Add the flour, yeast and salt to a bowl.

02 Gradually pour in the beer, a little at a time, and mix with your hands as you add it until you have a dough.

03 Knead the dough for about 10 minutes on a lightly floured work surface until lovely and smooth. Have patience because bread dough is a little sticky.

04 Transfer the dough to a greased silicone loaf tin/pan. Place it on the air fryer basket/crisp plate in the cooking pot.

05 Press prove on the multicooker, set the temperature to 35°C/95°F and prove for 60 minutes.

06 When the hour is up, if using steam bread, remove the fryer basket/crisp plate and pour 240ml/8½fl oz/1 cup water into the cooking pot. Return the air fryer basket/crisp plate. If using the air fryer setting, there's no need to add water.

07 Press steam bread or air fry, set the temperature to 180°C/360°F, and cook for 20 minutes.

08 Leave to cool slightly, then cut into slices, spread with butter and serve.

With Cheese If you want to add some cheese on top of the dough, sprinkle it over the top of the loaf 4 minutes before the end of the cooking time.

Without the Beer If you want to make the loaf without beer, simply swap the beer for the same quantity of warm water, like with our bread dough recipe on page 192.

Strong Bread Flour Versus Plain Flour You can either use strong bread flour or plain flour when making bread. We kept this as a budget recipe so used plain flour.

EASY GARLIC & ROSEMARY FOCACCIA

When we visited the Greek island of Crete a few years ago, I remember an Italian restaurant we ate at most nights. They had the best cherry tomatoes and lots of fresh focaccia. I was in food heaven. So, when I was thinking of my favourite breads for you, focaccia was top of the list. Before you worry that it's hard to make, it's just Dom's trusted dough in a silicone tray with a bit of seasoning – and you're all set.

SERVES **8**
FUNCTIONS **PROVE, AIR FRY**
PREP **18 MINUTES**
PROVE TIME **60 MINUTES**
AIR FRY COOK TIME **10 MINUTES**
TOTAL COOK TIME **1 HOUR 10 MINUTES**
CALORIES **160**

260g/9½oz/1¾ cups plain/all-purpose flour
1½ tsp instant yeast
1 tsp salt
180ml/6fl oz/¾ cup warm water

GARLIC & ROSEMARY TOPPING
2 garlic cloves
1 tsp dried rosemary
2 tbsp extra virgin olive oil, plus extra for brushing

01 Add the flour, yeast and salt to a bowl.

02 Gradually add the warm water, a little at a time, and mix with your hands until you have a dough.

03 Knead the dough for about 10 minutes on a lightly floured work surface until lovely and smooth.

04 Transfer the dough to a greased silicone square tray. Place it on the air fryer basket/crisp plate in the cooking pot.

05 Press prove, set the temperature to 35°C/95°F and prove for 30 minutes.

06 Remove the dough from the air fryer and use your thumbs and fingers to make indentations in the surface like a typical focaccia. Return the dough to the multicooker to prove for another 30 minutes at the same temperature.

07 Meanwhile, peel and finely slice the garlic. Add it to a small bowl with the dried rosemary and oil, and mix with a spoon. Set aside.

08 When the dough has finished proving, press air fry on the multicooker and set the temperature to 160°C/320°F and the cooking time to 6 minutes. After 6 minutes, open the multicooker and spread the garlic and rosemary topping over the top of your bread with a pastry brush. (We add the garlic now, and not at the start, so the bread doesn't get too brown a crust and the garlic doesn't overcook.) Adjust the temperature to 180°C/360°F and cook for another 4 minutes, to give some extra colour to the focaccia. .

09 Leave to rest then, using a pastry brush, brush some olive oil on the surface of the bread, then slice into squares to serve.

IRISH SODA BREAD MINIS

To my late Irish grandma, why did you never introduce me to soda bread as a child? It's delicious! If, like me, you didn't discover soda bread until adulthood, then it's a yeast-free round bread, made using bicarbonate of soda (hence its name) and buttermilk or yoghurt (we use buttermilk to make it creamy). You can either steam bread or air fry. So that they'll fit into different-sized multicookers, we've made small versions, plus it means they cook more quickly!

....

SERVES 8
FUNCTIONS STEAM BREAD/AIR FRY
PREP 12 MINUTES
STEAM BREAD COOK TIME 20 MINUTES
TOTAL COOK TIME 20 MINUTES
CALORIES 124

....

- 260g/9½oz/1¾ cups plain/all-purpose flour
- 1 tsp bicarbonate of soda/baking soda
- 1 tsp salt
- 210ml/7½fl oz/1 scant cup buttermilk

01 Add the flour, bicarbonate of soda and salt to a bowl.

02 Gradually add the buttermilk, a little at a time, and mix with your hands until you have a dough.

03 Knead the dough for about 10 minutes on a lightly floured work surface until lovely and smooth.

04 Divide the dough between 2 × 15cm/6in greased round silicone cake tins/pans. Using a sharp knife, cut a cross into the top of the breads about 1cm/½in deep.

05 If using steam bread, pour 240ml/8½fl oz/1 cup water into the cooking pot. If using the air fryer setting, there's no need to add water. Place the air fryer basket/crisp plate in the cooking pot, place the silicone cake pans on top. If you have a small multicooker, you may need to cook them in batches.

06 Press steam bread or air fry, set the temperature to 160°C/320°F, and cook for 20 minutes.

07 Remove from the tins and leave them to cool slightly before enjoying with butter or Jorge's beans on toast (see page 50).

No Steam Bread? If your multicooker doesn't have a steam bread setting, you can swap it for steam bake.

Just Air Fry? Note that the cooking time and temperature is the same for steam bread, steam bake or air fry. So you can use your preferred function.

GARLIC BREAD CROUTONS

Here are two ways to make garlic bread with a tiger bloomer loaf. In this first recipe, we get the garlic butter party started with croutons.

SERVES **4**
FUNCTIONS **AIR FRY**
PREP **6 MINUTES**
AIR FRY COOK TIME **9 MINUTES**
TOTAL COOK TIME **9 MINUTES**
CALORIES **225**

55g/2oz/¼ cup salted butter
3 thick slices stale tiger bloomer loaf
1 tbsp finely chopped fresh parsley
2 tsp dried oregano
2 tsp garlic purée

01 Chop the butter into chunks and add them to a ramekin. Place the ramekin on the air fryer basket/crisp plate in the cooking pot. Press air fry or bake, set the temperature to 120°C/250°F and cook for 5 minutes or until just melted.

02 Meanwhile, cut the bread into chunky pieces. Transfer them to a large mixing bowl, along with the parsley, oregano and garlic purée.

03 When the butter has melted, carefully remove the ramekin from the air fryer and pour it into the bowl with the other ingredients. Mix well with a wooden spoon so all the croutons get a good coating of garlic butter.

04 Tip the croutons onto the air fryer basket/crisp plate, spread them out and press air fry. Set the temperature to 180°C/360°F and cook for 3–4 minutes, depending on how crispy you want them.

Stale Bread Works Best If you don't have any stale bread, leave fresh bread out on a clean worktop for 3 hours and it will dry out a bit.

10-MINUTE TEXAS TOAST

This fast-food favourite is double-thickness garlic bread that's flipped halfway through to give a good garlic coating on each side.

SERVES **2**
FUNCTIONS **AIR FRY**
PREP **6 MINUTES**
AIR FRY COOK TIME **10 MINUTES**
TOTAL COOK TIME **10 MINUTES**
CALORIES **442**

55g/2oz/¼ cup salted butter
1 tbsp finely chopped fresh parsley
2 tsp dried oregano
1½ tsp garlic purée
2 double-thick slices tiger bloomer loaf

01 Chop the butter into chunks and add them to a ramekin. Place the ramekin on the air fryer basket/crisp plate in the cooking pot. Press air fry or bake, set the temperature to 120°C/250°F and cook for 5 minutes, or until just melted.

02 Place the parsley, oregano and garlic purée in a mixing bowl. When the butter has melted, carefully remove the ramekin from the air fryer and pour it into the bowl. Mix well with a wooden spoon.

03 Use a pastry brush to brush the garlic butter onto one side of each slice of bread. Place the bread on the air fryer basket/crisp plate. Press air fry, set the temperature to 200°C/400°F, and cook for 3 minutes.

04 Using tongs, remove the slices from the air fryer, flip them over and brush the remaining garlic butter on the other side. Place them back onto the air fryer basket/crisp plate and cook for another 2 minutes at the same temperature. Serve warm.

See It on the Plate Check out these Texas Toasts served as part of the ultimate steak sharing tray on page 93.

TEAR & SHARE CHEESY GARLIC BREAD

Garlic bread with cheese reaches a new level with this tear and share recipe. Filled with garlic butter and topped with two cheeses, it's perfect for pulling apart because of the way it is prepped. It's sometimes called hedgehog bread, thanks to its shape.

....

SERVES **4**
FUNCTIONS **AIR FRY**
PREP **8 MINUTES**
AIR FRY COOK TIME **12 MINUTES**
TOTAL COOK TIME **12 MINUTES**
CALORIES **460**

....

2 tsp frozen chopped garlic
100g/3½oz/½ scant cup salted butter
1 tsp dried parsley
1 cob loaf
55g/2oz/½ cup grated mozzarella
55g/2oz/½ cup grated orange Cheddar

01 Place the garlic, butter and parsley in an air-fryer-safe container. Place the container on the air fryer basket/crisp plate in the cooking pot. Press air fry or bake, set the temperature to 120°C/250°F, and cook for 6 minutes, or until the butter has melted. Stir well.

02 Meanwhile, slice the cob as you would slice any loaf of bread, but don't go all the way through – leave a 2cm/¾in gap at the bottom.

03 Using a pastry brush, brush the garlic butter in between the slices, being careful not to break any.

04 Turn the loaf and cut across the slices. Again, don't go all the way through. These slices will create cubes of bread – all attached at the base. Brush the slices with the remaining butter. (We brush one lot of slices and then the other as it's quicker and easier than trying to brush each individual cube of bread. Think of it as your garlic bread hack.)

05 Place a layer of foil on the air fryer basket/crisp plate, then arrange the cob on top. Create an overhang of the foil, as that will make it easier to remove your garlic bread once cooked. Sprinkle the cheeses all over the top of the bread. Press air fry, set the temperature to 160°C/320°F, and cook for 6 minutes, or until all the cheese has melted. (You may need to adjust the cooking time, if the cheese hasn't completely melted.)

A Panzanella Base We often find that the very base of our tear and share garlic bread is left over, and it makes a perfect panzanella, or tomato bread salad. Simply tear up the bread and add it to a bowl with 4 teaspoons extra virgin olive oil, 1 tablespoon dried basil and 1 teaspoon garlic purée. Mix everything together with your hands, then tip into the air fry basker/crisp plate and air fry for 3 minutes at 180°C/360°F. Meanwhile, chop 4 tomatoes into eighths and tip them into the bowl that had the bread chunks, along with 1 finely chopped small red onion. Season with sea salt, add an extra sprinkling of basil and mix well with your hands. Tip the tomatoes and onion into a salad bowl and, when the bread is done, add the crispy bread to the salad, mix well and serve. You could use spare crusts or any stale bread.

SWEET TREATS

HOW TO PRESSURE COOK A STEAMED PUDDING

The most requested recipe for this book has been for steamed puddings. You use the pressure cooker button but it tastes just like a steamed pudding cooked in a pan. Of course, it is much less hassle than cooking a pudding in a pan – there's no need for string and you just use your multicooker accessories instead. Invest in a pudding basin and you're ready to make that pudding.

Why Pressure Cook & Not Steam? The pressure cook function mimics a traditional steamer in many ways and does the job faster than the steam setting. Just imagine, a steamed pudding in 40 minutes. There are many possible flavours of steamed puddings, but we are going to start by showing you a classic jam sponge, then reveal the legendary sticky toffee pudding.

CLASSIC JAM SPONGE PUDDING

For your very first steamed pudding using the multicooker, I recommend a jam sponge. Any flavour jam will do the trick, or you could swap jam for your favourite orange marmalade. You can rinse and repeat with other flavours as you get more confident.

SERVES **4**
FUNCTIONS **PRESSURE COOK**
PREP **8 MINUTES**
PRESSURE COOK TIME **40 MINUTES**
TOTAL COOK TIME **40 MINUTES**
CALORIES **315**

- 55g/2oz/¼ cup granulated sugar
- 55g/2oz/¼ cup unsalted butter, room temperature
- 1 large egg
- 100g/3½oz/¾ cup self-raising/self-rising flour
- 2 tbsp whole/full-fat milk
- 3 tbsp strawberry jam

01 In a medium bowl, beat the sugar and butter with a wooden spoon until light and fluffy. Add the egg and mix slowly until smooth. Add the flour with a fork and mix gently until well combined. Pour in the milk, a little at a time, and mix well to create a creamy sponge batter.

02 Grease a steamed pudding basin, then spoon the strawberry jam into the base. Cover the jam with the sponge mixture, then wrap the top of the basin tightly with foil.

03 Add the trivet/rack to the multicooker, then place the pudding basin on top. Pour enough boiling water in the cooking pot to reach a quarter of the way up the sides of the basin.

04 Secure the pressure cooker lid, set the valve to sealing, and cook for 40 minutes, followed by a quick pressure release.

05 Carefully remove the steamed pudding from the basin and serve with custard (see page 216).

DOM'S STICKY TOFFEE PUDDING

A comforting steamed pudding – perfect with toffee sauce.

....

SERVES **4**
FUNCTIONS **PRESSURE COOK**
PREP **8 MINUTES**
PRESSURE COOK TIME **40 MINUTES**
TOTAL COOK TIME **40 MINUTES**
CALORIES **390**

....

125g/4½oz stoned dates
120ml/4floz/½ cup boiling water
100g/3½oz/½ cup dark brown sugar
60g/2oz/¼ cup unsalted butter, room temperature
1 large egg
90g/3¼oz/⅔ cup self-raising/self-rising flour

01 Thinly slice the dates and load them into a jug. Pour in the boiling water and stir well. Set aside to soak for 1 hour whilst you get the other ingredients ready.

02 In a large bowl, beat the dark brown sugar with the butter until light and fluffy. Add the egg and mix slowly until smooth. Gradually add in flour with a fork and mix gently until well combined. Drain the soaked dates and stir them into the batter with a fork.

03 Grease a steamed pudding basin and load it up with the mixture. Wrap the top tightly with foil.

04 Add the trivet/rack to the multicooker, then place the pudding basin on top. Pour enough boiling water in the cooking pot to reach a quarter of the way up the sides of the basin.

05 Secure the pressure cooker lid, set the valve to sealing, and cook for 40 minutes, followed by a quick pressure release.

06 Carefully remove the steamed pudding from the basin and serve with toffee sauce (see below) and custard (see page 216) or ice cream.

DOM'S TOFFEE SAUCE

This toffee sauce is perfect for pudding, but leave it to cool in the fridge and it's the best-ever toffee fudge.

....

SERVES **6**
FUNCTIONS **SAUTÉ**
PREP **8 MINUTES**
SAUTÉ COOK TIME **25 MINUTES**
TOTAL COOK TIME **25 MINUTES**
CALORIES **817**

....

360ml/12floz/1½ cups double/heavy/thickened cream
400g/14oz/2 cups dark brown sugar
225g/8oz/1 cup unsalted butter
½ tsp vanilla extract

01 Add the cream, sugar and butter to the cooking pot. Press sauté and adjust to a medium heat. Let the ingredients melt as the cooking pot warms up, but do not stir at this point.

02 Grab the side handles of the multicooker and shake it around in a circular motion to prevent the ingredients burning (you shouldn't stir the sauce yet). Be careful as it is hot and you don't want to burn yourself.

03 When the mixture is bubbling and rising up the sides of the cooking pot, start to stir slowly. The darker the toffee sauce gets, the richer it will be. We usually take it off the heat just as it's changing colour. Once you're happy with the colour, press cancel on your sauté.

04 Add the vanilla and keep stirring. Place the cooking pot to one side on a chopping board or a heat-proof plate so the sauce can cool slightly.

05 Once cool enough to eat safely (note it will be very hot at first), pour the sauce over sticky toffee pudding or chill in the fridge to make fudge.

EASIEST-EVER BISCOFF CHEESECAKE

By using the air fryer for melting the butter and the Biscoff spread, and the steam bake function to bake the cheesecake, this is very easy to make. Grab a jar of your favourite biscuit spread, a pack of biscuits for the base and let's mix it together.

SERVES **8**
FUNCTIONS **AIR FRY, STEAM BAKE**
PREP **12 MINUTES**
AIR FRY COOK TIME **9-10 MINUTES**
STEAM BAKE COOK TIME **25 MINUTES**
TOTAL COOK TIME **34-35 MINUTES**
CALORIES **811**

BISCUIT BASE
- 75g/3oz/⅓ cup unsalted butter
- 1 × 250g/9oz pack Biscoff biscuits

CHEESECAKE FILLING
- 2 × 280g/10oz tubs full-fat cream cheese (we use Philadelphia)
- 1 × 390g/14oz jar smooth biscuit spread (we use Biscoff)
- 1 tbsp vanilla bean paste
- 85g/3oz/¾ cup icing/confectioner's sugar
- 2 large eggs
- 2 tbsp double/heavy/thickened cream

CHEESECAKE DECORATION
- 8-9 Biscoff biscuits

01 To make the biscuit base, place the butter in an air-fryer-safe container on the air fryer basket/crisp plate in the cooking pot. Press air fry or bake, set the temperature to 120°C/250°F, and cook for 5 minutes, or until the butter is melted. Meanwhile, bash the biscuits with the end of a rolling pin in a medium mixing bowl, or blitz them in a food processor or blender.

02 When the multicooker beeps, tip the melted butter into the bowl with the biscuit crumbs, and mix well with a wooden spoon. Spread the mixture into the base of a 20cm/8in springform tin/pan, pressing it down and making sure it's level. Set aside.

03 To make the cheesecake filling, place the cream cheese in a large mixing bowl and add most of the biscuit spread (save a heaped tablespoon for later). Using an electric hand mixer, whisk until fluffy and creamy. Add the vanilla and sugar, and mix again to combine. Crack in the eggs and pour in the cream, a little at a time, and keep mixing until it's all well incorporated. Pour the mixture onto the biscuit base and smooth the surface with the back of a spoon. Wrap the tin tightly in foil.

04 Pour 360ml/12½fl oz/1½ cups water into the cooking pot, then add the trivet/rack, followed by the cheesecake. Secure the lid on the multicooker, set it to steam bake, set the temperature to 180°C/360°F and cook for 25 minutes.

05 When the multicooker beeps, remove the lid and let the cheesecake cool completely in the cooking pot before removing the foil and placing it in the fridge for 12 hours, or overnight.

06 When you're ready to decorate, place the remainder of the biscuit spread in an air-fryer-safe container in the cooking pot. Press air fry or bake, set the temperature to 120°C/250°F, and cook for 4-5 minutes, or until almost melted and creamy like chocolate sauce.

07 Remove the cheesecake from the tin and place on a serving plate. Use a spoon to drizzle the sauce around the edges of the cheesecake – about 1cm/½in from the edge – allowing it to drip down to create a drip cake effect. Crumble some of the decoration biscuits and sprinkle these crumbs into the centre of the cheesecake. Cut the remaining biscuits in half and arrange them around the edge to decorate.

Steam Bake Backup Plans If you don't have a steam bake function, you can pressure cook for 30 minutes or air fry for 30 minutes at 180°C/360°F.

BACK TO CHILDHOOD APPLE CRUMBLE

One of my favourite desserts from childhood was apple crumble and ice cream or, when it was freezing cold outside, custard. I was picking the kids up from their weekly baking class the other day, when they had made apple crumbles. They were ready for the oven and the teacher had told them to cook them for 35 minutes. My first thought was, I bet I can do it more quickly in the air fryer! I managed to reduce it to 20 minutes and this is how we did it.

SERVES **6**
FUNCTIONS **AIR FRY, STEAM AIR FRY**
PREP **10 MINUTES**
AIR FRY COOK TIME **12 MINUTES**
STEAM AIR FRY COOK TIME **20 MINUTES**
TOTAL COOK TIME **32 MINUTES**
CALORIES **480**

4 medium apples
1 tbsp extra virgin olive oil
1 tbsp ground cinnamon
1 tbsp granulated sugar
1½ tbsp golden syrup

CRUMBLE TOPPING

260g/9½oz/1¾ cups plain/all-purpose flour
130g/4½oz/⅔ cup granulated sugar, plus extra for sprinkling
115g/4oz/½ cup unsalted butter
1 tbsp ground cinnamon
½ tsp mixed spice/apple spice

01 Peel and chop the apples into chunks, discarding the cores. Place the apple chunks in a bowl with the olive oil, cinnamon and granulated sugar. Mix well with your hands, then transfer to the air fryer/crisp plate in the cooking pot. Press air fry, set the temperature to 180°C/360°F, and cook for 12 minutes, or until the apples are tender.

02 Meanwhile, make the crumble topping. Add the flour and sugar to a bowl, then chop the butter into bite-sized chunks and add them, too. Rub the fat into the flour and sugar until it resembles coarse breadcrumbs. Add the remaining crumble ingredients and mix well.

03 Transfer the apple mixture to a round 18cm/7in ceramic dish. Drizzle in the golden syrup, then shake the dish so the apples are well coated in the syrup. Spoon the crumble topping over the apples and press it down. Sprinkle with a little extra granulated sugar.

04 Pour 240ml/8½fl oz/1 cup water into the cooking pot and add the air fryer basket/crisp plate, followed by the ceramic dish. Press steam air fry, set the temperature to 180°C/360°F, and cook for 20 minutes, or until golden on top to your preferred doneness.

05 Serve the crumble with vanilla ice cream or custard (see page 216).

CLAIRE'S CHOCOLATE CONCRETE CAKE

This recipe is dedicated to my best friend Claire. During the planning stages of this book, I asked her what recipe she would love me to include. The first thing she said was her school favourite, concrete cake, where it was served with pink custard. It was my favourite at school, too, so she didn't need to ask twice. Of course, lots of recipe testing had to happen... What you'll love about this school favourite is how quick it is to prep the cake. I just outsourced the custard to the hubby (see page 216).

....

SERVES **4**
FUNCTIONS **AIR FRY, STEAM AIR FRY**
PREP **8 MINUTES**
AIR FRY COOK TIME **5 MINUTES**
STEAM AIR FRY COOK TIME **15 MINUTES**
TOTAL COOK TIME **20 MINUTES**
CALORIES **741**

....

170g/6oz/¾ cup unsalted butter
150g/5½oz/¾ cup granulated sugar
225g/8oz/1¾ cups self-raising/self-rising flour
55g/2oz cocoa powder
1 large egg
1 tbsp vanilla extract
1 tsp icing/confectioner's sugar

01 Chop the butter into small chunks and place them in an air-fryer-safe medium bowl. Place the bowl onto the air fryer basket/crisp plate inside the cooking pot. Press air fry or bake, set the temperature to 120°C/250°F, and cook for 5 minutes.

02 Remove the bowl of melted butter from the cooking pot and add all the other ingredients, except the icing sugar. It's one of those great add-everything-in-one-go cake mixes. Use a wooden spoon to mix the ingredients together well.

03 Transfer the mixture into a greased 18cm/7in cake tin/pan and use the back of the spoon to level the surface.

04 Pour 240ml/8½fl oz/1 cup water into the cooking pot and add the air fryer basket/crisp plate, followed by the concrete cake. Press steam air fry, set the temperature to 180°C/360°F, and cook for 15 minutes, for a fudgy brownie texture.

05 When the multicooker beeps, lift up the lid, sprinkle the top of the cake with the icing sugar and carefully remove the cake from the cooking pot. Set aside to cool a little.

06 Meanwhile, add a few drops of red food colouring to some custard (see page 216), until it's the right shade of pink for you. We like a light pink. Run a butter knife around the edges of the tin to help release it, then serve the concrete cake with pink custard.

DOM'S CUSTARD

I can guarantee that when Sofia and Jorge are standing behind Dom when he's cooking in the multicooker, it's because he's making custard. They will probably be armed with food colouring tubes in their hands, too, secretly planning what colour the custard is going to become.

SERVES **6**
FUNCTIONS **SAUTÉ**
PREP **3 MINUTES**
SAUTÉ COOK TIME **20 MINUTES**
TOTAL COOK TIME **20 MINUTES**
CALORIES **187**

600ml/20fl oz/2½ cups whole/full-fat milk
6 large egg yolks
4 tbsp granulated sugar
1 tbsp vanilla bean paste

01 Press sauté on the multicooker and adjust it to medium. Pour in the milk and warm gently.

02 Meanwhile, add the egg yolks to a mixing bowl and, using a hand whisk, beat them well. Add the sugar and continue to beat until well combined.

03 Slowly pour the hot milk into the mixing bowl, whisking until well combined. Add the vanilla and transfer the custard back to the cooking pot. Stir until it has thickened and is the right consistency.

04 Press cancel. At this point, we usually get out the stick blender and give it one last mix. This will get rid of any lumps and make the custard incredibly smooth.

05 It's now ready for serving or for the kids to add their desired food colouring. Just a few drops will add a lot of colour! Try it pink with our concrete cake on page 214. Go deep green for St Patrick's Day, or why not dark purple or bright orange for Halloween?

Love Really Thick Custard? For each extra yolk added, the custard will become thicker. Add an extra yolk if you want it nice and thick, or to rescue it if you feel it's overly thin.

TRAVELLING POPCORN

We have taken our pressure cooker and multicookers on many road trips. When we're staying at a cottage, in a caravan or a lodge, they always come with us. What they are particularly wonderful for is making a big pot of popcorn when you're having family time of an evening, using the sauté function and a few simple ingredients.

SERVES **4**
FUNCTIONS **SAUTÉ**
PREP **3 MINUTES**
SAUTÉ COOK TIME **15 MINUTES**
TOTAL COOK TIME **15 MINUTES**
CALORIES **202**

1 tbsp coconut oil
2 tsp unsalted butter
115g/4oz popcorn kernels

01 Press sauté on the multicooker and adjust it to high. Add the coconut oil and the butter and wait for the sizzle. Stir them until fully melted.

02 Add the popcorn kernels and make sure they are well coated in the buttery oil, then wait for the first one to pop.

03 Once the first kernel has popped, place the lid on the cooking pot (no need to secure it) and listen. When they start popping a lot, after about 2 minutes, press cancel on the sauté (this will stop them sticking).

04 When you have not heard a pop for a couple of minutes, the popcorn is ready for serving. Remove the lid, pour into bowls and enjoy.

INDEX

A
apples: back to childhood apple crumble 212
    jazzy apple sauce 74
    pork & apple burgers 78
asparagus: asparagus bundles wrapped in bacon 133
    mushroom & asparagus baked eggs 44

B
bacon: asparagus bundles wrapped in bacon 133
    bacon sandwiches on the rack 48
    big batch bacon & lentil soup 152
    Sofia's BLT pasta salad jars 158
baked beans on toast, Jorge's 50
banana chips, super-crispy 30
barbecue baked beans 50
barbecue chicken drumsticks & corn 64
beans: cheese & bean toasties 50
    Jorge's baked beans on toast 50
    taco mixed bean soup 152
beef: date night spaghetti & meatballs 162
    dehydrated roast beef 34
    garlic bread topped lazy lasagne 165
    Greek beef jerky 36
    how to steam roast with the probe 70
    Irish beef stew & dumplings 86
    leftover beef massaman curry 88
    the 2½ hour dried steak 36
    ultimate steak sharing tray 92
    Vietnamese-style steak noodle bowls 180
beer: weeknight beer bread 194
bifanas, quick 75
Biscoff cheesecake, easiest-ever 210
bread 190–203
    bacon sandwiches on the rack 48
    cheese & bean toasties 50
    Dom's bread dough for everything 192
    easy garlic & rosemary focaccia 197
    garlic bread croutons 201
    garlic bread topped lazy lasagne 165
    garlic cheese toasts 148
    Irish soda bread minis 198
    Jorge's baked beans on toast 50
    make-ahead Mediterranean strata 47
    panzanella 203
    proving 19, 192
    quick bifanas 75
    steaming 19
    tear & share cheesy garlic bread 203
    10-minute Texas toast 201
    weeknight beer bread 194
broccoli: broccoli-crusted salmon 98
    creamy broccoli Cheddar soup 145
bubble & squeak 120
burgers, pork & apple 78
butternut squash: butternut squash & sweet potato soup 142
    Kyle's butternut squash risotto 176
    my mum's super-slimming chunky soup 146

C
cabbage: bubble & squeak 120
    creamed cabbage & leeks 130
cake, Claire's chocolate concrete 214
Caribbean summer veg with rice & peas 188
carrots: fennel & thyme hasselback carrots 133
    my mum's super-slimming chunky soup 146
casseroles and stews: Irish beef stew & dumplings 86
    leftover pork cider casserole 76
    patatas bravas casserole 124
    vegetable stew with cheesy dumplings 136
cauliflower: cauliflower mash 121
    creamy butter chicken & yellow rice 172
cheese: cheese & bean toasties 50
    cheesy dumplings 136
    creamy broccoli Cheddar soup 145
    Dom's cheesy potato cakes 123
    garlic cheese toasts 148
    garlic Parmesan chicken wings 66
    prawn & halloumi orzotto 100
    tear & share cheesy garlic bread 203
cheese biscuits: Cheddar cheese chicken thighs 66
cheesecake, easiest-ever Biscoff 210
chicken: barbecue chicken drumsticks & corn 64
    Cheddar cheese chicken thighs 66
    chicken katsu curry 182
    chicken Kyiv, chips & garlic butter peas 62
    creamy butter chicken & yellow rice 172
    garlic Parmesan chicken wings 66
    kitchen cupboard pasta bake 160
    marry me family chicken pie 56
    multicooking a whole chicken 54–5
    paprika roast chicken 54
    salsa chicken rice box 168
    steam roasting with the probe 70

chickpeas: 10-minute Moroccan-spiced lamb steaks 185
chips 112–13
    chicken Kyiv, chips & garlic butter peas 62
    garlic mussels & frites 106
    lasagne chips 165
    steam air fry chips 113
    sweet potato chips 78
    ultimate steak sharing tray 92
chocolate concrete cake, Claire's 214
chorizo: chorizo peas 92
    Lancashire hotpot with a twist 82
    make-ahead Mediterranean strata 47
    mixed seafood paella 108
    patatas bravas casserole 124
cider: leftover pork cider casserole 76
    must try cider gammon 81
Claire's chocolate concrete cake 214
coconut milk: coconut lime jasmine rice 166
    coconut rice 188
cola gammon, must try 81
cream cheese: creamed cabbage & leeks 130
    creamy mushroom sauce for everything 74
    easiest-ever Biscoff cheesecake 210
    5-minute pasta sauce 156
    marry me family chicken pie 56
cress: egg mayo & cress jacket potatoes 118
crispy curried kale 131
croutons, garlic bread 201
crumble, back to childhood apple 212
curry: chicken katsu curry 182
    crispy curried kale 131
    leftover beef massaman curry 88
    naan bread curry 172
    prawn curry in a hurry 105
    Sofia's curry paste 172
custard, Dom's 216

D

date night spaghetti & meatballs 162
dehydrating 18, 26–37
Dom's bread dough for everything 192
Dom's cheesy potato cakes 123
Dom's custard 216
Dom's quick steamed eggs 44
Dom's sticky toffee pudding 208
Dom's toffee sauce 208
dried fruit: cooking times 30
dumplings: cheesy dumplings 136
    Irish beef stew & dumplings 86

E

eggs: Dom's quick steamed eggs 44
    egg mayo & cress jacket potatoes 118
    make-ahead Mediterranean strata 47
    mushroom & asparagus baked eggs 44
    rosemary & thyme Scotch eggs 91
    ultimate boiled eggs 91

F

fennel, garlic roasted 131
fennel seeds: fennel & thyme hasselback carrots 133
fish 94–109
    how to steam fish 96
    20-minute lemon pepper fish goujons 103
    see also individual types of fish
focaccia, easy garlic & rosemary 197
French onion soup, 20-minute 148
fruit: dried fruit cooking times 30

G

gammon, must try diet cola 81
garden salad 91
garlic: chicken Kyiv, chips & garlic butter peas 62
    dried onion & garlic 33
    easy garlic & rosemary focaccia 197
    garlic & herb roast potatoes 117
    garlic bread croutons 201
    garlic bread topped lazy lasagne 165
    garlic cheese toasts 148
    garlic mussels & frites 106
    garlic Parmesan chicken wings 66
    garlic roasted fennel 131
    tear & share cheesy garlic bread 203
ginger: maple ginger salmon packets 186
goujons, 20-minute lemon pepper fish 103
granola, nut-free autumn 43
gravy, hidden veg 59
Greek beef jerky 36

H

halloumi: prawn & halloumi orzotto 100
ham: ham & cheese cakes 123
    must try diet cola gammon 81
herbs: bits & bobs dried mixed herbs 32
    garlic & herb roast potatoes 117
honey glazed parsnips 134
hotpot: Lancashire hotpot with a twist 82

I

ingredients 20
Irish beef stew & dumplings 86
Irish soda bread minis 198

J

jacket potatoes, egg mayo & cress 118
jam: classic jam sponge pudding 206
jerky, Greek beef 36
Jorge's baked beans on toast 50

K

kale, crispy curried 131
katsu curry, chicken 182
kebabs, Portuguese pork 75

kitchen cupboard pasta bake 160
Korean-style barbecue marinade 64
Kyiv, chicken 62
Kyle's butternut squash risotto 176

L

lamb: how to steam roast with the probe 70
    Lancashire hotpot with a twist 82
    shepherd's pie with meaty mash 85
    10-minute Moroccan-spiced lamb steaks 185
Lancashire hotpot with a twist 82
lasagne, garlic bread topped lazy 165
leeks: creamed cabbage & leeks 130
    slow-cooked leek & potato soup 151
leftovers 70, 75–7, 88
lemons: 20-minute lemon pepper fish goujons 103
lentils: big batch bacon & lentil soup 152
limes: coconut lime jasmine rice 166

M

maple ginger salmon packets 186
marry me family chicken pie 56
mash: cauliflower mash 121
    mustard mash 120
    root vegetable mash 121
massaman curry, leftover beef 88
meat 68–93
meatballs, date night spaghetti & 162
Mediterranean strata, make-ahead 47
milk: overnight creamy yoghurt 40–1
Moroccan-spiced lamb steaks, 10-minute 185
mushrooms: creamy mushroom sauce for everything 74
    dried mushrooms for stock 32
    mushroom & asparagus baked eggs 44
mussels: garlic mussels & frites 106
mustard mash 120

N

noodle bowls, Vietnamese-style steak 180

O

oats: nut-free autumn granola 43
    overnight oats 43
onions: dried onion & garlic 33
    20-minute French onion soup 148
orzotto, prawn & halloumi 100
overnight creamy yoghurt 40–1
overnight oats 43

P

paella, mixed seafood 108
panzanella 203
parsnips, honey glazed 134
pasta 156–7
    date night spaghetti & meatballs 162
    5-minute pasta sauce 156
    garlic bread topped lazy lasagne 165
    kitchen cupboard pasta bake 160
    pasta sauce 160
    prawn & halloumi orzotto 100
    quick pasta for any occasion 157
    Sofia's BLT pasta salad jars 158
patatas bravas casserole 124
peas: Caribbean summer veg with rice & peas 188
    chorizo peas 92
    garlic butter peas 62
peri peri sweet potato wedges 114
pies: marry me family chicken pie 56
    pork casserole mini pies 76
    shepherd's pie with meaty mash 85
popcorn, travelling 217
pork: date night spaghetti & meatballs 162
    leftover pork cider casserole 76
    pork & apple burgers 78
    Portuguese pork kebabs 75
    quick bifanas 75
    steam roasted pork & crackling 73
Portuguese pork kebabs 75
'pot in pot' white rice 170
potatoes 110–25
    bubble & squeak 120
    chips and frites 106, 112–13
    Dom's cheesy potato cakes 123
    egg mayo & cress jacket potatoes 118
    garlic & herb roast potatoes 117
    Irish beef stew & dumplings 86
    Lancashire hotpot with a twist 82
    leftover beef massaman curry 88
    leftover pork cider casserole 76
    marry me family chicken pie 56
    mustard mash 120
    patatas bravas casserole 124
    potato wedges 114
    root vegetable mash 121
    shepherd's pie with meaty mash 85
    slow-cooked leek & potato soup 151
prawns/shrimp: mixed seafood paella 108
    prawn & halloumi orzotto 100
    prawn curry in a hurry 105
puff pastry: marry me family chicken pie 56

R

raisins, 54-hour 30
rice: Caribbean summer veg with rice & peas 188
    chicken katsu curry with sushi rice 182
    coconut lime jasmine rice 166
    creamy butter chicken & yellow rice 172
    how to cook 166–7, 170–1

Kyle's butternut squash risotto 176
maple ginger salmon packets 186
marinated salmon & vegetable rice 175
mixed seafood paella 108
'pot in pot' white rice 170
salsa chicken rice box 168
vegetable rice 171
risotto, Kyle's butternut squash 176
rosemary: easy garlic & rosemary focaccia 197
    rosemary & thyme Scotch eggs 91

S

salads: balsamic salad 47
    garden salad 91
    panzanella 203
    Sofia's BLT pasta salad jars 158
    tomato salad 123
salmon: broccoli-crusted salmon 98
    maple ginger salmon packets 186
    marinated salmon & vegetable rice 175
salsa chicken rice box 168
sandwiches, bacon 48
sauces: burger sauce 78
    creamy mushroom sauce for everything 74
    creamy seafood sauce 106
    curry sauce 88
    Dom's custard 216
    Dom's toffee sauce 208
    5-minute pasta sauce 156
    hidden veg gravy 59
    jazzy apple sauce 74
    pasta sauce 160
    spicy Spanish sauce for everything 124
Scotch eggs, rosemary & thyme 91
seabass, 5-minute spiced 96
seafood paella, mixed 108
shepherd's pie with meaty mash 85
soda bread minis, Irish 198
Sofia's BLT pasta salad jars 158
Sofia's curry paste 172
soup 138–53
    big batch bacon & lentil soup 152
    butternut squash & sweet potato soup 142
    creamy broccoli Cheddar soup 145
    my mum's super-slimming chunky soup 146
    no-prep creamy vegetable soup 141
    paella soup 108
    slow-cooked leek & potato soup 151
    taco mixed bean soup 152
    20-minute French onion soup 148
spinach, creamy wilted 130
squash *see* butternut squash
steamed puddings 206
    classic jam sponge pudding 206
    Dom's sticky toffee pudding 208
stews *see* casseroles and stews
sticky toffee pudding, Dom's 208
stock cubes, Sunday dinner frozen 61
strata, make-ahead Mediterranean 47
Sunday dinner frozen stock cubes 61
sweet potatoes: butternut squash & sweet potato soup 142
    peri peri sweet potato wedges 114
    sweet potato chips 78
sweetcorn: barbecue chicken drumsticks & corn 64

T

taco mixed bean soup 152
tear & share cheesy garlic bread 203
10-minute Moroccan-spiced lamb steaks 185
10-minute Texas toast 201
thyme: fennel & thyme hasselback carrots 133
    rosemary & thyme Scotch eggs 91
toasties, cheese & bean 50
toffee: Dom's sticky toffee pudding 208
tomatoes: creamy butter chicken & yellow rice 172
    dried tomatoes to tomato purée 33
    Jorge's baked beans on toast 50
    make-ahead Mediterranean strata 47
    mixed seafood paella 108
    panzanella 203
    patatas bravas casserole 124
    Sofia's BLT pasta salad jars 158
    tomato salad 123
travelling popcorn 217
turkey crown, simply the best 59
the 2½ hour dried steak 36
20-minute French onion soup 148
20-minute lemon pepper fish goujons 103

V

vegetables 126–37
    Caribbean summer veg with rice & peas 188
    hidden veg gravy 59
    marinated salmon & vegetable rice 175
    no-prep creamy vegetable soup 141
    root vegetable mash 121
    vegetable rice 171
    vegetable stew with cheesy dumplings 136
    see also individual types of vegetable
Vietnamese-style steak noodle bowls 180

W

weeknight beer bread 194

Y

yoghurt 19
    overnight creamy yoghurt 40–1

THANK YOUS

Fans and our growing community We love you all! Thank you from the bottom of our hearts for telling us your struggles and what you want us to cook, so we can give you what you really want. We appreciate every social media share, every nice review and comment, and we can't wait to bring you even more recipes.

Our eldest son Kyle He is the third piece in our day-to-day business puzzle. We have you behind the scenes, and most people don't realise the hours you put in helping the business grow. Along with all the trips to the supermarket you do when we have run out of an essential ingredient, you are also so talented, and we wouldn't be where we are now without you. You make us so proud and always have done.

Our daughter Sofia We can never thank you enough for all your help in making this cookbook. All the times you cooked a recipe for us, tested an ingredient, helped with the washing up, designed our herbs and spices drawer, or were happy to help whenever we needed you. We couldn't imagine making this book without you. We are so proud of you and what you have achieved and continue to achieve. Go girl!

Our boy Jorge Mummy's biggest-ever foodie fan. Well, you asked me to make another cookbook just so I could cook 12 different things a day for you and here it is. It has more of your favourite things and recipes you helped us make. You may be the baby of the family, but it didn't stop you helping and we are so proud of you.

Sarah Thank you for being our everything, our recipe tester, our sounding board and our friend. We love your eagerness to try new recipes and get stuck in, and how your feedback shapes our recipes within the pages of this book.

Claire Thank you for being our biggest cheerleader, trying all the food and giving us the encouragement when we needed it the most, and for all the school runs and early morning recipe talk. You're so kind and we couldn't ask for a better best friend and we can't thank you enough.

Our agent Clare Thank you for all your help and support over this book and the previous two, and for reminding us that we can say no and that things must be right. And for believing in us and making this great book happen.

Denise They say it only takes one to say yes. You were our yes that started our cookbook career, and we love working with you to make beautiful books with great recipes. We love your ideas, your efficiency, your beautiful writing style and your amazing experiences that shine through in the cookbooks you publish. Thanks for believing in us again and making this cookbook a reality.

Nicky Thank you for being our feedback machine – for being there on every day of the food shoot, sharing your thoughts and making the text and the photographs even better, and for working alongside us to turn our recipe ideas into a reality.

Christina We feel so lucky and privileged to have you as our food stylist. We love that we can share our vision with you and you can turn it into beautiful food with gorgeous props. We threw you in at the deep end and you rose to the challenge.

Sophie Wow, we have loved every moment working with you. Your lovely smile and eagerness to please. From your organisation to your delicious foodie spreads on the shoot, we just didn't want it to end.

Alison Loving your beautiful product photos and how they help the reader learn how to use their new multicooker. I've always loved working with you, and you're so talented as well as being a great friend.

Dan Thank you for your great photography and your attention to detail, and for flicking up on the screen one of the photos when I just wanted another look.

Georgie Here we are on a third book with you. We love your design and get excited each time the templates come back with your latest vision and inspiration.

Jo Thank you for being my dream editor – for making me sound better, for transforming our basic recipes into something grand and for your attention to detail. We love your way with words, your organisation, being our person and putting up with all our crazy edits, on our journey to making the best book we can. You have such a beautiful editing style that I am sure our readers will love.

ABOUT THE AUTHORS

Sam and Dom Milner live in East Yorkshire in the north of England with their three kids, Kyle, Sofia and Jorge. Their home is oven free and surrounded with all their favourite kitchen gadgets. Sam met Dom when he worked as a sous chef more than 25 years ago and they love cooking together with their gadgets.

For more kitchen gadget recipes, handy tips, recipe videos and easy-to-follow tutorials check out:

KITCHENGADGETSCLUB.COM

If you have any multicooker recipe questions or just want to say hi then our socials are:

- thekitchengadgetsclub
- kitchengadgetsclub
- thekitchengadgetsclub
- kitchengadgetsclub

ALSO FROM SAM & DOM MILNER

The Complete Multicooker Cooking Guide

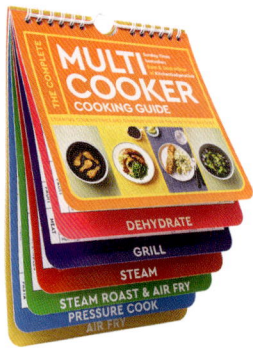

The ideal companion to this book, featuring essential cooking times and temperatures by function for the most popular foods.

The Complete Air Fryer Cooking Guide

Perfect if you want to focus on air frying, this contains more than 275 of the most popular cooking times and temperatures.

Both of these really helpful flip-over charts can be hung up in your kitchen or attached to your fridge with the magnetic sticker provided.

And for more air fryer recipes and techniques, try our air fryer cookbooks.

The Complete Air Fryer Cookbook

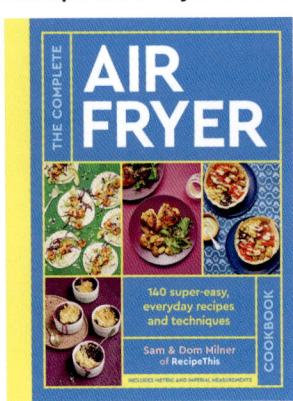

The *Sunday Times* bestseller

Air Fryer Easy Everyday

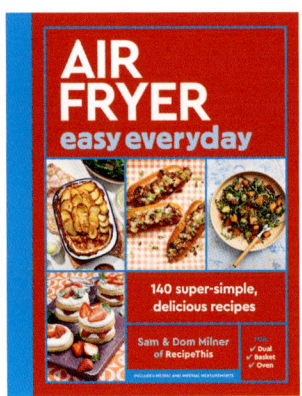

Super-simple air fryer recipes with instructions for both dual and basket machines.